SOME

other books by the author

POETRY
Dawn Visions
Burnt Heart/Ode to the War Dead
This Body of Black Light Gone Through the Diamond
The Desert is the Only Way Out
The Chronicles of Akhira
The Blind Beekeeper
Mars & Beyond
Laughing Buddha Weeping Sufi
Salt Prayers
Ramadan Sonnets
Psalms for the Brokenhearted
I Imagine a Lion
Coattails of the Saint
Abdallah Jones and the Disappearing-Dust Caper (illustrated by the author)
Love is a Letter Burning in a High Wind
The Flame of Transformation Turns to Light
Underwater Galaxies
The Music Space
Cooked Oranges
Through Rose Colored Glasses
Like When You Wave at a Train and the Train Hoots Back at You
In the Realm of Neither
The Fire Eater's Lunchbreak
Millennial Prognostications
You Open a Door and it's a Starry Night
Where Death Goes
Shaking the Quicksilver Pool
The Perfect Orchestra
Sparrow on the Prophet's Tomb
A Maddening Disregard for the Passage of Time
Stretched Out on Amethysts
Invention of the Wheel
Sparks Off the Main Strike
Chants for the Beauty Feast
In Constant Incandescence
Holiday from the Perfect Crime
The Caged Bear Spies the Angel
The Puzzle
Ramadan is Burnished Sunlight
Ala-udeen & The Magic Lamp (illustrated by the author)
The Crown of Creation (illustrated by the author)
Blood Songs
Down at the Deep End (with drawings by the author)
Next Life
A Hundred Little 3D Pictures
He Comes Running (chapbook)
Miracle Songs for the Millennium
The Throne Perpendicular to All that is Horizontal
The Soul's Home
Some

THEATER / THE FLOATING LOTUS MAGIC OPERA COMPANY
The Walls Are Running Blood
Bliss Apocalypse

SOME

poems

•

10/25/98 - 4/25/99

Daniel Abdal-Hayy Moore

The Ecstatic Exchange
2014
Philadelphia

Some
Copyright © 2014 Daniel Abdal-Hayy Moore
All rights reserved.
Printed in the United States of America

For quotes any longer than those for critical articles and reviews, contact:
The Ecstatic Exchange,
6470 Morris Park Road, Philadelphia, PA 19151-2403
email: abdalhayy@danielmoorepoetry.com

First Edition
ISBN: 978-0-578-14335-4 (paper)
Published by *The Ecstatic Exchange*,
6470 Morris Park Road, Philadelphia, PA 19151-2403

Cover art by the author
Back cover photograph © Lou Wilson

DEDICATION

To
Shaykh ibn al-Habib
(and the continuation of the Habibiyya)
Shaykh Bawa Muhaiyuddeen,
all shuyukh of instruction and ma'arifa
and
Baji Tayyaba Khanum
of the unsounded depths

✺

*The earth is not bereft
of Light*

CONTENTS

Some Good Advice Thrown Out   9
Some First Light   11
Some Leaves Fall   12
Someday   13
Some Deaths   14
Some Cries from the Heart   15
Some Indications   17
Some Observations   19
Some People   21
Some Days   22
Some Words of Reassurance   24
Some Trees   26
Some Prayers   29
Some Tears   31
Some Steps   33
Some Sad Sounds   35
Some Sights   37
Some Things Left Unsaid   38
Some Incomprehensible Words   40
Some Vision   42
Some Cries   44
Some Proof   46
Some Instructions   48
Some Minor Miracles   50
Some Attempts at Intimidation   53
Some Purposes   56
Some Solutions to What's Insoluble   58
Some Glimpses of the Dancer   60
Some Definitions of Love   61
Some Flashlight Beams   63
Some Mournful Notes   65
Some High Ringing Sounds   69
Some Flutterings   71

Some Love Thoughts   72
Some Serious Advice   79
Some Demon Detractors   82
Some Insectivore Transformations   84
Some Shaft of Light   87
Something About Sleep   89
Some Softly Falling Rain   91
Some Moments of Expansion   93
Some Thoughts in the Air   94
Some Mysterious Transformations   96
Some Simple Explanaton   100
Some Mischances   102
Some Late Night Positioning   104
Some Words to the Heart   106
Some Poetry   108
Some Abyss of Light   110
Some Recollections   111
Some Morning   113
Some Vision of Prayer   115
Some Sand Grains   117
Some Story   119
Some Coordinates   123
Something   125
Some Trick   127
Some Artifacts   130
Some Matter   132
Some Details   134
Some Last Wishes   135
Some Flute Music   137
Some Shops   141
Some New Dimensions   143
Some Random Notes   145
Some Opalescent Gleams   150
Some Great Souls Have Passed By   151
INDEX   154

It has been related from the Prophet, *salallahu alayhi wa sallam*, that he said: "God Most High says: 'If I know that my servant is overwhelmed by obsession with Me, I cause him to desire to implore me and to confide in Me. If the condition of a man is such, then he loves Me and I love him. And if the condition of a man is such, and he desires to be forgetful of Me, I come between him and his forgetfulness. Such men are My saints in truth. They are the true heroes. They are those for the sake of whom, when I will to punish the people of the earth, I set the punishment aside.'"
— Abu'l-Hasan 'Ali b. Muhammad al-Daylami
(A Treatise on Mystical Love, page 9.)

SOME GOOD ADVICE THROWN OUT

When an obstacle comes
throw out the obstacle or throw out
"when an obstacle comes."

When an opening comes
throw out the opening. Throw it into
where it came from.

When a space of joy comes
throw out the space so only the joy remains.

When the galloping horses of love come
throw out love and
climb on the horses and ride them to the nearest
lake of love and ride them across the
lake into the night of love where their
solitary hooves can still be heard
echoing forever in the deep
forests of love.

Throw it all out,
obstacle opening joy love,
throw each one out
into where they came from,
go there yourself,
throw out yourself
into where you came from,

be there for a fraction of a fraction of a second,
fish of light swim overhead,
fish of darkness,
something so deep,
something so inexplicably deep,
the heart held in space by such fragile
   particulars

this body —
throw it out,
this light —
throw it out,

throw out
"throw it out"

10/25

SOME FIRST LIGHT

I lay my body down.
Light occupies its place in space
   aslant the brown town.
I leave a bone in the room.
The bone blooms. It's got buds now,
buds of love, fuchsia petals hanging down.
Color in the dark corner.
Red of fuchsia against black.

O the town's music draws me out
like the whistle of a single tone.
The room is now the whole world
filled with bloom.

I can't go on. It draws me back.
Out and back incessant rhythm
like a bone xylophone.
Death and life and life and death
occupy a single zone.

I lay my body down before the wakeup call
that calls each soul back home.
When I will leave my bone
in a dark place.
Go on alone
where first light shone.

SOME LEAVES FALL

for Mohja Kahf

Some leaves fall spiraling down.
Some leaves fall lopsidedly zigzagedly down.
Some seem to fall like plummets straight down.
Some twist and spin as they fall down.
Some seem to take their sweet time sailing down.
Detach themselves, fall through the air, land at our
    feet, from their treetop heights,
bronze and dry, down, down,

falling through the morning air, crisp clear
October air, crisp golden petal-like leaves
showering individually down,
some at a rakish slant,
some tumbling acrobatically down,
little leaves Galileoly racing big ones down,
all adding mulch to the glittery forest floor,
however they came down,

awed me, catching my breath as I see ones as if
    for me especially
falling right in front of my eyes, however
    mathematically calculable their
fall, making a
  spectacularly humble finale

down.

10/26

SOMEDAY

One of these days we'll round a corner
and it'll be perfect, same place,
but perfect.

Trees going straight up, gnarled but hopeful,
clouds like thoughts, empty but illumined.

Or the corner will round us
and we'll see it's already perfect as it is,

pangs of pain and anguish, physical
    pain, mental anguish,

offsetting the very grand scale of our
inner worlds, whose pure helium

bursts the seams of our physical beings
at dream level.

                                                     10/29

SOME DEATHS

When the body dies and faith becomes a
    burning ball of light
suspended in the air, increased in size with
    every breath, until the
whole world becomes engulfed in it, light
in windows, light on tables and chairs,
everything an object of love, how could God

take a body in torturous pain, cancer or stroke,

but if we crawled to the woods by a tree and
waited for death there peacefully,
deer unafraid of us, songs of birds our
    bursts of breath, our burning eyes their
flight, at world's edge

in day or night, faith larger than life
with our eyes and ears in it
flickering in its flames, watching our

arrival at God's gates, hearing His words.

10/30

SOME CRIES FROM THE HEART

Hang my heart out on a line to dry, it's too
    waterlogged with love!

Let migrating birds feed at its tissues, peck at its threadbare
sinews, muscles grown tired clenching and
unclenching love's impossibilities, love's
letdowns, loves all-too-human
buckets of cold water thrown on the heart's
    natural fires.

Take it out of my body like bread from an oven, still
    raw after all these years! Still too
glutinous!
I can't just sprinkle dry flour on top and pretend it's
    cooked, or strew
sesame seeds in a pattern that spells, *"I give up!"*

Ah, but it's in none of these places, it's still inside my
body like a drunk, vowing to
clean up its act and go sober once and for all,
the next minute swigging the sweet golden
lips of the bottle's mouth like an
enraptured duck!

Torn to shreds, patched together with tape,
torn apart again—will it

finally become latticework to see the true

heart of hearts, secret-most heart, God's only,

there in a
green shade, pearly fountain, splashing

contentedly in the sun?

10/31

SOME INDICATIONS

The journey gets more perilous,
a dice cup and seven lost sergeants,
   the Ouija Board fell overboard,
ice has formed on the hull, the stern and the
   mast, ice in the shape of flames, icy
red, raw-tipped, incandescent to behold,
I'll shout out when we reach the shore.

We'll never reach shore. We're
   too far out. The earth is a ball.
Astrolabes are rusty things, they
   squeak when turned. The
compass became befuddled, threw away its
apron and dove in among the dolphins.
They speed along.

I haven't taken one step forward, but a
few steps from side to side.
Someone up ahead in a nimbus of fog
with hands in perfect focus beckons me forward.
I step forward and the whole world
   dissolves beneath me.
This is no laughing matter. Yet is it
   laughter I hear
reverberating among the faraway stars? Or sobs?
What is our main sound?
For whom do we make it? We're

never alone. I'm with you in your faraway room,
watching you write. You've just written
   all this down. A
tiger lurks among the nouns. Serpents among the
vowels. In green profusion
vines among the verbs display exotic blooms.

Here's an uncharted place. I expect the
local shaman may greet us in
any disguise he pleases. Howls. Leaps from the page.

I just rolled zero, and my train's pulled in.
Each window displays a different face.
Each face is a round expressive eloquence
with flashing eyes.

I began alone. I go it alone.

End alone.

Will you come along?

                                                11/1

SOME OBSERVATIONS

I think that when you start out writing a poem because you
   want to, you end up with
less than you did before you started.
A kind of white wall comes up, a landscape
   frozen solid of flying cranes in triangular
formation with a village below of
large dwarves, all of whom own small
entrepreneurial businesses retailing combs to
the cat populations who generally prefer

good grooming. *See what I mean!* It's absolutely
pointless, and not particularly beautiful. Not as

beautiful as, say, the way your lips move when you
talk, or the quizzical glances you give me after saying
you can't quite figure me out, what I'm
doing, you haven't gotten a
handle on it, and my lame attempts at
explanation suddenly realize, in their
own threadbare way, that it's not an

explanation you want, it's a
demonstration. Meaning in action.

Tall tree trunks with their shadow perpendiculars
catching fire all at once like
birthday candles on a cake. Your
eyes so full of life, so utterly

seeing, as if all pupil, where vision enters,
flips upside-down, seeps along nerves and

becomes song.

11/4

SOME PEOPLE

Some people write their desperation on the wind.
My love for you is close to grief.

I've seen the purple alligators slap their tails,
pigeons take off all at once like a single hand.

What opens the heart is a thin key made of
   imperishable stuff.

We can't know when it'll fall into our hands.
How wide the heart will open once it's turned.

One look or word or soul in a body so perfectly attuned
     is enough.

What opens the heart is a thin key made of
   imperishable stuff,

but sears through the soul like a flash flood or forest fire
which is one part national disaster one part desire.

What falls after through the air as ash is a perfect leaf.
My love for you is close to grief.

11/4

SOME DAYS

It started on a Monday. First the
roar, then the waves, then the rollers.
The surf lifted the furniture. Lamps flickered.
Fish could be seen swimming in the kitchen.

Then Tuesday rolled around.
Ferns shot up between the floorboards. Exotic
birds roosted in the rafters. I glimpsed
what I thought were the Three Graces all in
pearls and mother-of-pearl, shimmering against
late morning light.

Wednesday brought flames. Non-burning ones, flames of
thought and mental fire, flames of
intuition, flames of desire. All
colors of the rainbow. Flickering like eyelids
overcome with passion, suddenly snapping open
to gaze on a superlative vision of godhead,
   intimations licking into images, fiery
lanes up through space to the holiest
precincts.

Thursday darkness, velvets of shade dropped over
chairs in cool rooms. Darkness
visible, that kind of thing. A warmth to it.
As if moving through water.

Friday was crystals and roadways and the

charms of wildlife freely flying through the air or
scurrying along the ground, darting under
houses, stealing fruit from the orchard, so we'd be

walking at leisure and come upon the debris of shells and
skins left haphazardly on the trails.

Saturday lifted off the earth, and we thought it
might be for good, we'd never return to the
train station which is our
lives departing from the visions of our innermost
hearts. Saturday was
best, sailing like fresh laundry on a line,
    drenched in sunlight, fluttering
        blue and yellow shadows against
wind-pulsed pockets of air in its natural
        propulsions.

Sunday was the putting-it-down-into-words,
symbolic and inaccurate, like a
small high window in a deep, dank room
where a single ray tries to illuminate it to its
corners, but ends up with one long
lateral ray to the floor, through which motes more
transparent than our very lives fall slowly, in no
hurry to land, so that at

times they look suspended, immobile in space, while at
other times they seem to float up.

11/7

SOME WORDS OF REASSURANCE

"For one condemned to death, you sure seem sprightly!
You wear the color yellow on your head,
your dogs are sleeping peacefully, nothing seems too
   urgent for you. I wish I had your
calm."

"Calm seas, broken pipes.
Fire fills the window.
I've had great conversations with ants.
I'll tell you the story of how the
   blind princess solved the
wizard's puzzle one day.
Slam the door in no one's face
who has reason to love you.
Yellow? This old hat? Van Gogh the painter
left it on a chair.
He shot himself. Couldn't
   become his paintings.

Welcome to the bird's nest.
I'll tidy up the day I die.
Enter the tomb a pauper, all debts paid.
I've a couple outstanding.
Money can't buy them.

Sit down, you look a wreck.
I know the date I'll die. You're
navigating in the dark.

How do I know?

It's written."

11/8

SOME TREES

Bells are strung on the innermost trees,
raccoons wear their facemasks backwards.
The scurrying you hear might be them
or it might be angels.
The sky is a deep purple. The earth a deep green.
Hardly anyone comes here any more, and it's
    off limits to most.
I've seen the solitary reveler out the
    corner of my eye on especially windy
Thursdays. I've seen a

rooster enter the woods and come out
a well-dressed man with a perfect seam in his trousers,
on his way to a successful career in
marketing. They say it's

enchantment, and the right snap of the fingers
will make it all disappear just like that,
so I pray nobody snaps them.
Without these trees the world would be
cheapened, like original things at a Thrift Store.
I've seen the nightmares of some people
come in here for a rest.
The hectic electricity that goes up the
    spinal vertebrae of the dreamers
and syncopates their bones,
crackling out to their nerve ends until they
wake up,

gets abated when their nightmares lean against these
opal tree trunks for a minute, to maybe
   smoke an odd cigarette.

And I've seen the good dreams come in here too.
Once a whole troop of classical players in
green buckskin roared in, rehearsing their lines
"trippingly on the tongue," but became so
relaxed that out of their shadows small antelope does
were seen carefully placing their hooves on the
forest floor, and
     darting away.

The roar you hear's only the ocean. It's
red and gold, and carries the
twig raft with the lizard on it and hundreds of seeds of
exotic vegetation to faraway islands.
Life is expansive. I feel it in my heart that

beats from gloom to gladness within seconds
when I glimpse the central pool, like
quicksilver uncoiling in the darkest center of the
forest, like a pearl on black velvet.
No vision of peace lasts for long, however,
unless you enter it the way a body enters a
frogman's suit, to the ends of its fingers and toes, completely,
and you walk away in peacefulness
utterly at peace, doing all your accustomed
   acts with a peaceful symmetry
bringing some to fruition with flowers, some with
statuesque perfection with stones. And all with God's

light glance upon them, like the

rays that come fluttering through the bell-strung
    trees here to illumine
a motion so subtle you might doubt it
ever took place.

                                              11/9

SOME PRAYERS

To the long shed in darkness
   at the bottom of the hill
send horses of light.

To the long-suffering, bent,
charwoman on a stairs in Berlin
send angels.

To the stunned navigator on the
high seas who's in despair of finding port,
send waves of peace.

To you, O soul of my soul, light of my heart,
send the black rose that awakens the dead,
the white rose of plenitude,
the yellow rose of delirium,
the green rose of forgiveness.
I'm finished with disbelief, and I'm
   in the clouds.

We're surrounded by a blinding whiteness
that stretches from sky to sky
and from earth to earth.
I don't know what I'm doing here.
I'm lost without God.

To the green plant in a dark shade
send bell-shaped flowers.

To the lips of my beloved,
send the taste of strawberries,
    ones not plucked
from tainted ground, but from the
pure blue snow on the high Alps of transcendence,
one bite of which floods my beloved's eyes with
sights of the Garden.

Send a dark rain to the glass forest.

Let its bells resound.

                                                          11/12

SOME TEARS

A little green dragonfly comes to my side
and wants to be my bride.

Its sweet face looks at me with dragonfly eyes
but we're so different in size.

I am a lumbering inert human being
and it flies.

"Ah thing," I say, "sweet thing, love
is something we have little control of.

You may not have wanted to be with me
so seriously."

It hovers a little whirring its rainbowy translucent wings.
"Patience and true love sometimes bridge

impossible things."
"Can I become dragonfly, you transform into human?"

But something takes place between us that is truly luminous.
I can't explain it. Winds blow and winds abate

but this wind only increases
and incubates.

It has its dragonfly world it goes to and I to mine.

Can I say in both worlds God's single sun doesn't shine?

What a sun! Look at its grandeur, its silver disk!
"Love is nothing," the dragonfly says, *"unless you take risk."*

But it's a dragonfly, and I'm a man, without wings.
Will I be able to reconcile these seemingly irreconcilable things?

What a sweet green dragonfly it is! I want it so badly.
Can this love I have for it really end sadly?

One moment it's near with its sweet face whirring close to my eyes.
Then it flies off to its dragonfly paradise

where I cannot go. I cannot go. I'm a man.
It's times like this I sometimes regret being a man.

11/14

SOME STEPS

A boy holds a very precious gold fish (spectrum-speckled, feathery, gorgeous)
in a clear pool of water, cupped in his hands, fingers tight so it
won't leak,

steps off from one place onto another as he goes,
walks a long curvilinear distance, trees go past,
roads congested with cacophonous activity slide under him,
enters tall Baroque buildings and goes through their echoing corridors out the
back entrance, carrying this

fish which never blinks, doesn't
swim in such shallow water, but
waits patiently to be carried to its
destination somewhere
under the sun, anywhere where he can
do the free breaststroke, swim in circles, vibrate,

the boy's hands become oceans, his
body coral reef, his thoughts tropic
   breezes as he
enters his house through a
door the size of the Taj Mahal, through an
entry hall as silent as Napoleon's tomb,
up a flight of stairs as
gradually momentous as Marc Anthony
mounting the forum steps to address
his fellow Romans, turns at the

top of the stairs and goes down a hall and
plops his fish in a round fish bowl as big as the world

where it swims in silent calligraphic figures all though the
night and keeps on swimming

into day, on and on and on in sweet calligraphic figures
through the bright day.

                                                                                                          11/19

SOME SAD SOUNDS

Out on the edge of night a
   violin plays all by itself.

Its song so sad rivers stop rippling
to listen, pinecones stop
dropping.

Everything on edge, heads cocked, hearts
   cocked to listen.

A tall black girl comes singing into the picture, a deep sad song.
She's got a hat on her head as big as a house.
The furniture inside is
covered with white sheets.
It sits on the edge of an ocean, black and white
waves hitting the xylophones of the rocks.

Some creatures make room for other creatures.
Some snap and show rows of tiny pointed teeth.
On such a night streaks flash across in the sky,
while underneath the sad violin goes on playing,
and I open my mouth to join in their song
equal to the sadness in the strings. But my
   mouth stays open, silent, hands crossed over my
     heart.

I've let all the reindeer loose in an endless blue light.
They flowed out through my legs like water

rejoining the sea.
I turned my back on civilization and nothing changed.
Bats make that fluttering paper sound in the
    night, paper fluttered in panic.

But the night is long and absorbs every sound into its
deep magnanimity,

even if sorrow is longer, and seeps into the
long grass to the sloping valleys below.

11/20

SOME SIGHTS

My love for you is such
that my heart is a shivery vase of icy water.

Every time the train passes by it shivers.
The window blackens. The stars go dark.

The world shudders.

Doors in nowhere open. Space expands.
Flowers bloom in the night. Exude rich syrups.

The black house at the end of the road catches fire.
No one's there. Shadows get flesh and sit in chairs.

Conversations become cosmic. *"Pass the salt"* becomes
"God says: Be! And it is."

A colt is born in a cold barn.
A grassblade is born. A sunbeam catches it

and holds it close.
The world purrs.

11/21

SOME THINGS LEFT UNSAID

I haven't said it and I have said it.
It falls between the words,
freefalls through miles of wilderness sky like sparks.
The latticework of its shadows frames the
   unmomentous phrase and gives it
an epic feel, surrounds an indifferent gesture
with magnified meaning.

How can you put love into words? It has enough light to
illuminate New York and go on into
outlying fields and woods, where no one's
been before. Its light goes into the
deepest inner crevices of
twitch-nosed creatures with weak eyes.
Follows equally down a dirt road behind a horse.
Slants across every sharply defined
detail of twig, briar and spider web embedded in the
black velvet throw of night.
Hovers in air until morning, catching
each drop left on the spider's thread with a
pinpoint of light making each droplet stand out
like cut glass.

At this the citizens become delirious and
incapable of their normal routines,
their hearts both heavier and lighter than normal,
moving around inside their chests like
thinking entities that enter with the

caution of a courteous intruder

capable of violence. As capable of
violence as of song. As capable of
song as of violence.

11/22

SOME INCOMPREHENSIBLE WORDS

I woke you up and you were
    incomprehensible.
You spoke the language of stones, salt flats,
sunlight on rushing water. Your words were

vines across space, ants up tree bark, dark shadows
cast in the depths of caves.
Your words melted ice. Were cachés of
seeds for arctic birds. Pots of pomade
behind latticework windows. Incomprehensible

but melodious drops of water in cisterns
in sun-drenched deserts.
Small mammals curled up in nests, hungers of
fledglings. I don't know to this moment

what you said, you were a night watchman holding his lantern
aglow in a very black night, like a
detached planet burning in our atmosphere,
like a call for help or a reply of assistance
where none was expected.

Your voice was like coiled rope, like
    oil rolling across rock, like an
ancient song a shaman might sing before
    going into trance.

I would launch my boats on its waters.

I would stand on its shore and wait for
exotic water birds to pluck fish from its
depths. Heart-depths. Of a soul

emerging from sleep. Love-depths. Of a soul
opening its lips before comprehensible
words could form comprehensible sentences.

I tuned my ears to a similar frequency.
I heard the clear call of the loon,
the clear call of the sky in which
each of us is born.

The clear call of God to
come to Him.

11/27

SOME VISION

> *God is in the opinion of His slave.*
> — Tradition of the Prophet
> (salallahu alayhi wa sallam)

With all due respect,
You are a healing God, Who lifts two
halves and makes them one again.
If a branch is broken before its time
the two parts either become complete in themselves or they're
somehow joined together again.
Things work themselves out by Your Vigilance and Grace,
and Your purple and black oceans of turbulent night
become sunlit with gulls and pure white
clouds again. Your

daylight floods our pores from both
outside and in, our patience rewarded,
Your infinite Mercy upon us, no
Light as broad or as warm as Your
God-Light, as completely

showering throughout creation,
each green plant on gold stem of it, each flower
radiating joy, up from the ground the same as
starshine from out in space millennia before finally and
tactilely reaching us, our hearts the true

terminals and origin pools of it, O God, Your
extension without limit, Your love unstinting,

even death faces you with its single white face and smiles, enters Your
Light willingly, like

gnats disappearing in sheets of summer day, microscopically and busily
entering the light with full faith in it, we all do,

so needful of Your Embrace,
You give it to each of us, the
order of the day done, the all-encompassing

Compassion only You can encompass with
to turn us totally and
completely to You, O God,
Healer and Maker whole,

Uniter of all,

God of love over all.

11/28

SOME CRIES

I peer down into the long pond
and the whole world comes up to meet me.
World leaders in their limousines,
high class criminals in designer clothes,
divas and dunces, successful poets with
lifetime grants and published volumes,
historians with agendas, ballerinas with
sprained ankles, gas-drinkers, pop-blowers,
boomers and spandex careeners, glop and soup of
psyche both human and inhumane, the
waltz of life in 4/4 time—an extra beat for the
dimension of the unknown—when I would

rather have bent down and found
a banquet of high conversationalists whose eternal
subject was the Divine Ray in its various manifestations,
elevated quips and quotations from
luminous scrolls, each phrase illustrated with
3-D examples from real life, saucer-shaped
spark-outlined objects moving through space
to display the total grandeur. Elegant

rainbows tied in small knots around the
details. Narrations of harrowing spiritual
adventures past where both
fire and ice hold sway.
The edge of night. The antediluvian antechambers of day,
resonating with that curiously comforting

creature sound found at zoos, cries from the
peacocks, hungry roars and the
chittering of small mammals. Birds, flocks and
whole communities of birds, from peewees to
raptors, hawk-eyed in their corners waiting
for the signal to swoop.

I peer down into the long pond
and see Your Name form in the foam.
And hear Your Name called on the
     fine edge of things.

O God, I call out Your Name
on the fine edge of things.

                                         11/28

SOME PROOF

"Produce your proof, then, if the
elegance you speak of is
capable of existence in this
world."
I pulled out a matchbox, pushed open its little drawer,
and there sat my dragonfly, shimmering and
twitching its long dark body
like a sliver of amethyst,
its oblong wings lying softly on its back
more translucent than stained glass.

It turned up its face to me, all eyes.
Face from the moon of Phoebos, planetoids on the
dark rim of our galaxy, eyes twin domes of lapis,
eyes whose complexity would astound the most
accomplished mathematician, who, having
cracked their structural code, would still be
incapable of creating them.

My dragonfly lifted its front legs into
angular takeoff position.
I knew it wanted to speak, to
introduce itself and represent its
inner beauties firsthand. For without
a true picture of the stirring thoughts and
cosmic landscapes in my dragonfly's heart
how would anyone know the real
depth of its treasure?

"I have one short life here, gorgeous wings on each side,
move forward at great speeds, am
capable of inflicting serious bites.
I love skimming ponds for delectable
tidbits. Skim and dart, circle and zoom.
That's my delight!
Your world is a shade and a
poor place compared to mine. Can you watch your
own shadow flying under you across the surface of
ponds?" And with that
my dear dragonfly
zoomed away.

I looked up at my questioners, their
jaws agape, their hooded eyes a fraction less hooded.
They'd witnessed something
flash before their eyes with the golden flame of life all
   around it, the hallowed halo of
     sweet existence, ecstasy in a
living gem zooming through space.

My dragonfly performed various aquatic sports and
dragonfly gymnastics, looping the
   loop with upside-down flight,
flawlessly returning upright.
It hummed as it zoomed. Modern drone-like
   electronic tunes. Its innocent

face monopolized by those goggly futuristic eyes,

almost smiling.

11/29

SOME INSTRUCTIONS

South is where my boat lies. We'll
    head south.
Don't disturb its hull of breath and sighs,
its hull of fragile nothing-much-but-air.
I don't know why I think it'll get us there.
It sits on a purple tide, reflected back
by the mercury water it sits in, inch by inch.
Bring compass, book and astrolabe.
We're heading out to open sea, and more.
Days'll go by, gulls and bitterns all the
    birds we'll see, an occasional
octopus, squid rising like heartbeats,
descending like thoughts in the boiling mass,
an occasional albatross, spreading its
    tent-like wings.
Did you bring binoculars, faith, the certitude we'll need
to ever see shore again? We're pushing far from
lights and city roofs, horizons of
anything but waves. Waves and more waves,
that's where we'll be, resting on God's
waves to bring us home. Home more than a

hot hearth or warm face, more than a
hill with a house on it, a full garage.
Home where the sky parts, where God's rays emerge.
Home inside-out to what you see here,
silent beyond silence, bright beyond light.
Home not slow-motion to here, nor speeded up,

but things come to birth in all their perfect gestures there
and fold into grace again like a flickering of light
folded upon folds of light and darkness
back into original stuff, in folds of the heart.

Voices on the waters will guide us in,
calls across emptiness
more than we'll need to turn —
but turnings's not what we'll do, but go out in one
long trajectory past all the straits we've
ever traveled before, heading way past before us, way past
any notions even of distance, even of
endurance.

Pass the butter, pass the water, let's sit back and
set sail.

I feel it rise beneath us. I feel the heart's hull
unfurl.

12/1

SOME MINOR MIRACLES

He took a green rose and dipped it in silver
    until it became red.
He rode a giant white horse through the night
until it became a house
with seven stories and enough room for a
family of bears, a family of ruthless Mongols,
a family of Swedish immigrants intent on
    farming the New World
and one blind alchemist whose hands alone,
passing over nondescript objects, could change
hard hearts to gold.

He walked across a bridge until it became
a city of quadrilateral buildings and
    trapezoidal lights.
The dazzle was almost beyond what his
human eyes could bear.
He turned to the identical twins, one of fire and
    the other of lead, and
asked them three questions: One: *"What are the
other two?"* Two: *"What is the third?"* And
Three: *"Why are we here?"*

The sky's mouth opened and stars poured out
into the palm of his hand.
He counted them slowly onto the usurer's table.
Each coin became a tiny stallion
    galloping off in a different direction

mane of ice mane of lavender mane of sharp blades
carving the night into a free-standing sculpture
of each of us naked under a full moon representing
our actions and their inner motivations
before the bloody tribunal.
I've seen their expressions, and
   hoped the angels of their better natures
would triumph when it came
time to pass judgment on our indiscretions.

He stood in the same place for many miles.

He said the same sentences in the same silence.

He thought aloud what others had only
   thoughtlessly said to themselves.

He moved his legs as if they belonged to
      someone else.

He wore the antlers of indifference until they
wouldn't fit between trees.

He ran with wolves over a
   moonlit landscape frozen over in a
single chord of music.
Their cries, one after another, crowded the night
with their plaintive sound, woke
the chemical elements from their sleep, so that
at last the formation of a structure whose
sacred dimension was perceptible to all

could take place on earth, and
crowds gathered for all those who
survived the flood, and Noah too,

and his smile, when at last the green
    rose became red,
lit up the world.

12/6

SOME ATTEMPTS AT INTIMIDATION

They sat him down in the back of the van
and spoke Welsh.

Welsh is as good as any other language
to confuse his mind.

He wore his golden slippers, covered in mud,
to hide them.
They put a fist in his face, a
burning mattress, a hill of crosses, a
pistol, a picture of a pistol, a
recording of a pistol going off.

They gave him fire to drink.
He drank it.
They put a house on top of him.
He lived in it.
They tried to turn him into a wild beast.
He turned into twenty, forty, two hundred
wilder beasts than they could ever imagine,
but each one purred, played ball with its
paws. Licked its coat.

They sat him down in the back of the van
and spoke Welsh.
He spoke Welsh back, in perfect sentences.
Except he spoke better Welsh.
His Welsh had The Ocean Epic, The Golden

Torch Story, The Way to Break Horses.
His Welsh opened doors all along the street
onto warm kitchens and eiderdown beds.
His Welsh didn't talk back.

They spoke Russian.
He danced all night in the village square
to the sounds of accordions.
They made a bonfire, but he fell as sparks.
They staged mock battles with real armaments.
He danced the dance of the clown who's been
turned into a rabbit by a sorcerer, and who
digs a tunnel through the middle of the
earth out the other side onto green fields and
golden sunlight.

He wore his golden slippers that never let him down.
They called out to him for help on the high seas.
He helped them, but more than that.
They became kings on their own islands.
They called for his head on a silver platter.
He brought the platter, opened the cover
and his head opened its mouth and sang a tune.
The tune made them sweat, made them dizzy,
    then giddy.
They started laughing uncontrollably. They
  peed all over themselves. Rainbow colors.
They found themselves up to their necks in their own
      pee.
Their eyes were frightening. Their laughter stopped.
The head kept singing.

The lyrics went something like this:
One, two, fly to Timbuktu.
Three, four, ceiling hits floor.
Five, six, cover me with sticks.
Seven, eight, I just can't wait.
Nine, ten, never again.
They understood and begged for mercy.
They got it.

They sat him down in the back of the van
and spoke Welsh.
He looked scared. He looked right at them.
His look was so strong it created
an angel between them, bronze muscular
lightningbolt that killed them.

They sat him down in the back of the van
and spoke Welsh.

The night was bigger than both of them.

God bless them.

12/6

SOME PURPOSES

The purpose behind the wheel that moves the
    colossal boat-like apparatus,
that shivers the rope with live vibrations, that
actually makes baby pines push up their
    tiny spears, then their lances, then the great
trunks of their spreading domains, then they
groan and whisper in the wind,

the infinitely fine and intentionally even finer-tuned
purpose behind the way masses of people move
individually through a mass, across the
continent westward or eastward until they're
shielding their eyes with the flats of their hands against the
glare of hard sunlight bounced off the
surface of the sea,

the way tiny beads of moisture gather on glass then
slide down to the bottom, the way

butterflies unaccordion themselves out of cocoons then fly
for days south along Ecuador, Peru, Chile and around the Horn,

there's a clear purpose somewhat obscurely kept from us
behind large white sheets for day and large black sheets for
night, and if the purposes for each event or
each creational articulation were too
obvious we might lose heart, we might lose
interest, though the

purpose be of a radiance no physics can measure,
with a rustling of visible wings, a flight across the open plains of
beasts like giraffes who scissor their
motions with such grace it brings
tears to our eyes.

                                                                             12/10

SOME SOLUTIONS TO WHAT'S INSOLUBLE

1

The pole doesn't reach to the bottom,
    weeds are clotting our progress, the
bronze disk of the sun bears down like a
    surgery done in an emergency,
and there's no sure way out.
The phone rings, or the cavalry appears on the
horizon a thousand strong, horses
    snorting for battle.
Words fail me. I keep trying to articulate
around a principle, or assemble enough tangible
building blocks of words that a given
subject is adequately, even superbly, defined,
but there is also a high wind.
Words can't be
heard distinctly in such a high wind. And there's
no sign of it abating.
We trudge on.

2

How many angels on the head of a pin,
in a puff of smoke, the twinkle of an eye,
in a simple declarative sentence? Angels
    everywhere, filling space with a sense of
spaciousness. Dancing between house plants,

skating without skates over the surface of water.
Finishing what's been left unfinished in mid-air.
Sending love beams from one heart to another
and finding ways to make them take up
    permanent lodging there, in the
middle of a luxuriantly landscaped park.
Looking at hopelessness and circumstantial
stalemate, and saying, in angelic thought patterns no
human can reproduce, *"Let's see what we can do!"*
And doing it, by the permission of God.

And getting it done.

                                              12/14

SOME GLIMPSES OF THE DANCER

The dancer, like a flame-tip, flickered in the air.
The courtyard was of alabaster. The sea of light.
Birds sang the day away. The dancer danced.

Flies buzzed and gnats did aerial choreography
unseen by most and under-appreciated by all.
The sultan raised his hand and ships appeared
with billowing sails approaching shore.
Pirates flashed white teeth on leathery skin.
The weather changed. Blue shadows fell.

The dancer turned and disappeared, then just as
suddenly appeared from behind a pillar, still
turning, face a brown flower, body more
thought than body, concatenated series of
fluid gestures,

fluttering eyes, song an animal might
sing. Shifting moonlight. Swirling sand.

SOME DEFINITIONS OF LOVE

Love is the answer to a question posed long ago in
   childhood when no one was listening and the
sun was already setting out the window in the
darkening living room. I was all

alone in the room, the house was silent and brown,
the outside noises had died down, and I
posed the question for the first time with my
whole soul and body, and it's just now, at
58, beginning to be answered, bells at

angles in an arched window peal in
opposite directions as swallows fly in diagonal
lines across white sky.

Love is a small bottle with a round-topped stopper
tipped over slightly, thick purple ichor inside
beginning to slide out.

Love is the call from one hillside to another on a
sunny day, sheep climbing the hill as if
sideways, lambs baying, dogs barking,
a car horn far away sounding and
resounding down the long valley.

The professor of love absented himself from the
conversation because, he said, his studies were
all theoretical, and he'd
never been in love to the best of his knowledge.

But the swinger of scythes knows about love,
and the wader in swamps.
The circus performer understands both its
momentary nature and its lack, and has to
content himself with a few seconds of weak spotlight.

But the one who lays down, who lets
salt water rush over him, the one who
runs across a city at night for no known or
knowable reason, until his legs ache and his
heart's about to explode in his body like a
pomegranate fountain spraying its
glassy seeds, knows about love.

Love is an afterglow and a prelude. It's also
the pain of the universe holding back its reply
until we've shed everything, our bones walking
out of our bodies, and recognition takes place in a
place where no recognition has
    ever taken place before. I want to

call out until the walls ring. I want to
cry out until the beasts have returned to their
caves in the hills. Until the birds have
gathered. And the woods are still.

I let myself slowly down the rope of love.
Its bucket holds the ocean, moonlight reflected in it,
but may never reach dry land.

12/19

SOME FLASHLIGHT BEAMS

"Here. Take this flashlight. If it gets any darker
    turn it on."
"It can't get any darker. It's night."

"The beginning of the world was darkness. The
    end of the world is light."

"And what is in between then, coils and turmoil,
mountain upheavals, rainbows breaking into falling
debris, earthquake, flood and fire storms? Blight?"

"The intricate weaving love makes through the earth.
The umbilical's warp and the lung's woof, under and
over of the desperate textures of life."

"And all this ends in light?"

"A little of the light can be seen in the
things of this world, leap of sparks between
loving eyes, tremulous grips of the heart,
what words can do, fortuitous blind
meetings of two people on earth, feet unlike and
like each other, breath from the source, heartbeats
like forest fires crackling twig and bark, whole
fields alight as if by electricity, small
animals running in fear, running for
cover for the sheer joy of it. All this from the
love-beats that come in waves across the earth,

faces shatter and all that's left is their light,
eyes become palaces with endless corridors and
hearts become central gardens, and nothing's left
untouched by the rhythmic pulse of this light.

It begins in utter blackness. Planets emerge. There's
starlight. Then anguish and death. Torture and
pain. But it ends in light.
Meanwhile, take this flashlight.

If it gets any darker turn it on.

But when light comes, add yourself
   to the light."

                                                                       12/19

SOME MOURNFUL NOTES

> *Out of nature I shall never take*
> *My bodily form from any natural thing*
> — W.B. Yeats (Sailing to Byzantium)

1

The lover sees the Other in his eyes, and
    calls it love.
He searches dark corners, walks down
    long halls.
Love's fire burns blue then golden in the fields
until he's dry chaff, wishes he were
dry chaff, wishes he were wind that
takes dry chaff away,
drifts it along
tall mountaintops, diffuses it in turquoise sky
utterly consumed.

I'm tired of pissing and shitting, tired of the light of day.
Give me a darkness so black I'm gone, mouth
sucking like a fish's, perpetually puckered, eyes
    saucers, mind a blank, drifting in the
air, no longer caring where the
weight falls, where the night ends.

The walls are triangular, the ceiling round.
I'm falling through endless space with no sound.
I'll land before my heart does
in a place bereft of peace.
I'll wake the tavern keeper up before the dawn.

Is there no one left who's sane, who's had their
fingers burned?
My lips are caricatures of words.
My song is gone.
It's love that's played this trick on me all along.

Look! Ten rabbits hiding in the lawn!

2

I fear when I die there'll be a jug of fire on my bed,
a saucer of black grapes on my pillow,
my house a shack of wind and gray flakes,
my books empty, my pens full of sour blood
and my domesticated animals roaming free
    bellowing and lowing
as the sky rolls open like two sheets of lead
and a bare-back white horse canters down and
gallops past my bed but doesn't stop to
pick me up or let me
hang onto its mane and carry me to
       safety.

I've thrown over the anchor. My ship's adrift.
My deathbed looms before me like a ghost.
I see a face there that's my own and not my own.
Whose is it? All God's raptors blink with
    neutral eyes. Those eyes are
flying through a blazing sky, their pupils like tall
blackened trees, their crowns also ablaze. They swoop

    down on what's pure, white, shivering
in the snow, then swoop
up again. I've got my invocations to
keep me safe from harm.
I'm a white hare abandoned in a white field.

God, keep me warm.

3

But I haven't really seen anything like down yet.
Sawhorses haven't kicked me,
door knobs haven't resisted my touch,
the blond sheep of terror haven't grazed on my face,
the loop that goes sky-high then down past any known
horizon hasn't snatched me up and sent me on its way.
Have I known love at all yet, Lord?
Where are my tears of blood, my palsied hand?
Loss of appetite and the tossing and turning that has
no worldly relief? I

wake and Your All-Pervasive Name comes round me like the
three dimensions themselves. You've

become my space.

I go down the road and You're way ahead of me,
giving my actions meaning and
meaninglessness both. My heart thinks overtime.
It's replaced my mind for thinking.

My mind is trying to get warm on a steam grate
like the most destitute of men.
Most of the time it's just as well.
Other times, when the pendulum swings heavy in its case
I wish I didn't have any heart at all.

But You're the surgeon who put it there, Lord,
and You'll be the surgeon to remove it again.

So sing to it. It will only
listen to Your song.

When love's hit it with this much force,
it can only respond to Your song.

12/27-28

SOME HIGH RINGING SOUNDS

When I fall in love I'm dashed to the ground,
    a fly hit by a swatter.

My heart feels like an anvil after it's been clanged.
The elegant empress wants a brooch
and it's held up in fiery tongs.

The clang continues to resound.
Can its sound reverberate through the halls
to the central room?

It feels like suspended in space, cold mist
    closing in.

The empress is haughty, as befits an empress,
and wants it now! The brooch of fire and
jewels, to wear at her neck.

A dark town sinks further into the ground.
German Expressionist rooftops, moon like
    white sound.

My heart feels like an anvil, iron rising
    monolithically above ground.
Town sinks, heart rises, no one's around.

I would love to swim with dolphins in a green sea.
Swim away from all this. Swim free.

My heart feels like an anvil after it's been clanged.
Where's the hammer that hit it, who
    holds it, who wields it?

The clang hangs in the air like a name.
Who'll hold it as his own? Who'll endure the
    shame?

I'll go off with iron shoes down an iron road,
the sky clanging around me, red with flame.

Hello silence. Hold me.
I'll be good.

You needn't speak a word this time.

The empress has her brooch
and I have mine.

1/3

SOME FLUTTERINGS

Broken things litter the way, bones, bottles, little
pieces of being, all searching to be

united to the main shaft, the
major tree, the wind that

blows through the sacred yard, tightrope airwaves for owls,
the music the spheres make turning against

nothingness in silvery endlessness, that heavenly
squeaking sound of uttermost being

turning at its own pace in the space of a thought or the
blink of an eye before sights

enter it again with their populous
wings and fluttering ribbons, black and white

streamers igniting into
fiery rainbow colors at their ends

trailing long fingers through space
like notes of song.

1/6

SOME LOVE THOUGHTS

1

Little heart, to whom I direct these songs, like a
   gold harp on a high wall, like a
window gleaming across town, like
train wheels screeching late at night,
kewpie doll at a carnival, diamond behind glass
   mined by black hands, cut by
     European fingers, held up by
       no one now,
on display for anyone to see,
available in the air, fact of life, each facet shining,

each breath of my life laid out like a mat on the
road for you to walk on, my sweet one,
straw through which I sip the infinite in time,
magnifier of what is to what becomes
   monumental to the heart, I see suddenly

horses' heads, they're racing in one direction, their
   manes wild as surf, their eyes wide but steady,
heads in profile of horses going from right to left,
they'll all arrive more or less at once, my lovely one,
and be judged by your gaze, the tips of their
hot noses reaching the finish line first, then
the rest of them, like bodies slipping into invisibility,
disappearing into the unseen, last tail hairs
   pulled in behind, until nothing remains

but the sensation of speed and a furious energy,

from birth out of nothingness to entrance into
nothingness again, and I
watch it move, from right to left,
gone in a second, but

in that second black rainbows are born from a
single diamond, faces of love are born out of
blue smoke and open their eyes on death without
flinching or experiencing fear,

I hold up two mirrors, one facing forward, one facing
up, there are flames along the edges and
ice along the handles, and no one's face
appears in their depths, but

gardens do, and full fountains, and
exuberance, and their spherical arc meets
   somewhere over Antarctica, and the
grim geometry of their reflections, emptiness
    mirroring emptiness,
suddenly flowers in a tear that appears on the
petal of the rose I offer you in the pitch black of
   night, where no one can
     see it being

given and
none can see it being received.

2

I wish you were here with me, inside my skin,
looking out on a world
   definitely gone ashen,
definitely less picturesque now that you've
entered the arcade, your

space is so metaphysically brighter and the
world looks like a dull place, is a dull place
beside it. Yours is a space of thought-rockets, light
   detonations, speeches from
glistening toads and linnets, words heard audibly from
the mouthless elements lined up in a
chorus whose
   harmonies hang on the air, while the

world's elements fit snugly into the silence of death and
   extend it. The world's elements of

action and stillness are so much
   furniture shifted around, we
bump into, when the
   room's dark, but love, when you're

with me, inside my skin, your torrents and
tremendous gushing places, then action and stillness are

angelic beings chasing each other in play,
objects of the world transformed into

licking faces intricately fitted, each
    facing the Creator in its own way with

full throated song, as I do,
when you're near, inside my skin,
lighting it for me, lighting the long way
and the short, lighting, O my dear,

the difficult corridors.

3

Death is a kiss right on the lips that
   never ceases, the deepest
kiss of our lives, on luscious lips. They

glisten with a Vaseline sheen, it's a

space hitherto unknown to us that suddenly gets
an undeniably gorgeous set of lips. Then we're

drawn into its body, and out of our own.
White unicorn herds fan across the horizon, each
   one a perfect gem.

Death lies close by our sides and throws one
companionable arm over. It flows across us
like yellow waves. Why yellow?
For us it's black, for the Chinese it's maybe yellow,
or saffron, or the pink tinges in a jungle orchid,

the stellar touches on a petal's tip. Subtle.
Irresistible.

Death is more than a salamander in the sun bobbing its head
insolently up and down.
It's more than a trap door in space we
   never suspected would actually
      open.
It's a new world, longer than this one, for which
this one isn't even a mirror reflection, but only more like
a smirk in passing, hard to interpret if it's
ironic or mocking, but a smirk nevertheless.

Death is some rusted iron machinery in a
drafty barn. Late winter. Deep snow.
Nothing moving

but spirit.

4

What is the relationship between love and death?
Do they both walk a thin line? Do we

court them both with shy glances and brash advances
existing in our ticking mortal bodies while both
love's and death's winds blow,

hurricanes around an old house? They seem so

different, each difficult in a different way, each
with magnetic undertow we can do, it seems,
nothing at all about, nothing at all. Winds blow,

hundred mile-an-hour winds, taking the roof off,
the tops of our heads off, or our whole heads
completely, leaving exposed heart. Each

an enigma, one passionate as whirlwind,
 death passionless as fog, or bare light, flat
    light stretched
from horizon to horizon, and we glide
into it like a lover, face first,
sliding into its depths, it enveloping us like love does,
    so we
have limited movement, fragile almost or
furious, loving the way a workman might slam a
    sledge hammer down, death also a

hammer-blow on an anvil, one ring of metal on
metal all it takes, one

strike all it takes to make sparks fly.
And love flies, death lies flat,
love lies back, arches over
the beloved, is all
bending and cradling. The way

death finally cradles us like an all-loving
mother who will take care of us forever,
the way only love of God can, forever, love for a

mortal rarely having foreverness, yet sometimes an

emblem of it, the loving touch a

light hammer blow which death has no

part in, but a kiss also like the earth

opening for us and beckoning us

to enter.

               1/8-10

SOME SERIOUS ADVICE

Black butterflies fly through the night as
   invisible as breath,
white horses almost disappear in the
     ocean's foam.
A soldier, buried in the ground, will lose his
grimace after a time.
A ballerina, on tiptoes for years, will
     eventually come down.
But the sky feels nothing, it just rolls across whatever's there
the way time goes up one side of a redwood and
   down the other, pieces of fog stuck to its
eyelashes and perfect tiny claws.

Time is the expression on the face of an entire nation.
It is minute, evenly spaced holes in the porous
   epidermis of the butterfly that
     began this poem. She's

so elegant, her antennae are a pale mauve, she
sees the world in fitted sections, is
   attracted to scent the way
millionaires are attracted to travel, with a
   profligate intensity and
single-minded concentration.
Blindness is a dimension unto itself which
those who have sight can never imagine. It's
not simply the lack of something, but a
   condition of existence, the way a

caterpillar must molt its
furry brown outer skin before
emerging as a butterfly, either
    black or morpho blue, spreading frail
wings among the high and tangly
branches of a rain forest.

This poem has progressed to this point without even giving
one piece of serious advice, which makes, in a way, a
point about giving advice in the
first place, even to
yourself, though one can

often impart very important information to
someone which can either be
heeded or ignored, while red

billows surround the shoulders of the ingénue like
waterfall steam from the highest elevation
gradually descends across the
rocks and crags of the tropical
    gulch it pours down.
The ingénue's black and gorgeous, and spreads her
arms like butterfly wings as she
sings into a glittery silver microphone in a
thick nimbus of blue smoke, her
    silver gown accentuating the
dark creamy sheen of her skin, as her
eyes seem to flutter through the
      canyon of the moment and out into
          glaring sunlight,

she suddenly becoming visible after her long
passage through the night,

like white horses heavily frolicking in the
ocean's froth, riderless, almost wild again,
lifting noble heads above the boil and
    turmoil of the waves, nostrils
opening and closing, eyes
riding their height and staring
down as their front legs rise
   high into the air before they
dive back into the roiling waves.
Endless circles of activity coiling back and
out again from themselves, a black

butterfly fluttering through it all with that
enigmatic insect mask
expression on its face, a certain

neutrality its strength, frail
    thing through every
       circumstance, out
the end of every situation, boxed in then
free, inwardly, nowhere else to
go, certainly

not an easy matter, but a
freedom not, for us,
totally impossible to attain.

1/15

SOME DEMON DETRACTORS

Little red demons hammer my spine,
jaggy tails, red shower-caps with sharp red ears
    poking out,
prehistoric pincer-bone gnash-pigs
saw at my scapula, happily
grinning gash wizard beetle pookas, snappy
    black shirts and hairy fingers,
poke and poke at my pudenda, they're
talking high speed, no way to translate them,
sacroiliac sack-cloth flat burner sop poobahs
jump up and down repeatedly and even
more repeatedly on my coccyx and all
    attendant bone structures, slit-eyed pea green
butt-faced, silver-edged
    spike-haloed teeth pointier than
        rapier snarker-snookers, uglier than
fat toads, snap all my toe bones, stretch all my
finger bones, saw on my rib bones, what nasty
music do they play? Capper punk
dark blue razor-back snit-poopers with big
trunks they slam and slam on my
skeletal under-struts capitalizing on their
greater size and mastodon
strength compared with highly
intimidated me, snarked and totally pooka'd,
smash-beaked, poked to death and
spoon-fed to the fark-parker, snuffed in the
stash-marsher, mashed head first in the

smasher,

O I still hope to sing!
God bless my song!

No tunnel dredged body slicer fist-pounding
flash rasher, blood seeper, face pusher, corpse
    squelcher
squishes my soul! O love, I
clench you with my last teeth,
last fetid breath, last eyelash sweep!
Heart cinch you up with a
    golden string!
Loose you forever living eternally
through everything!

                                           1/16

SOME INSECTIVORE TRANSFORMATIONS

1

There's a strange cobalt lamp somewhere
and a large lizard sits at it
    writing this poem.
He wishes he were human and at peace.
His little forked tongue snaps out and in.
His sharp circle eyes flick forward and back.
He dreams of marshes and sunlight. He writes:

      "oligarchy mesotopes."

He studies the words without comprehending their
    meaning. But he's a
lizard and can't be expected to make any sense.
Or at least not any human sense, not
    yet at least, since he's only
hankering to be human, not yet shedding his
scaly skin to fully emerge as one.

A bronze blaze flares up before him.
A firefly of thought sits in the air inside the
    blaze. It shimmers as it
      turns. It casts a
pale glow on the air around it.
The lizard darts his head forward, flips out his tongue, and
snaps the firefly into his mouth and
    out of the air, leaving a momentary

firefly shape in the air behind it that floats for a
second then closes around itself and
disappears. So much for

thought the lizard thinks. And having
thought, notices at once he's a little less
lizard. A little more…

thoughtful.

2

Or, put another way, it's a

human under a leaf writing the
lizard's song, showing the spiritual
distance between lizard and human
in an attempt to suggest the great
almost Darwinian leap from normal human
mortal to living saint, who knows the

answer to the Unified Theory and the secrets of
Quantum Mechanics and the intermeshing
realities of string theory and how the

universes are strung together because saints know
personally Who strung them, Who

in an indefinable way, at the articulated touch of His will, made the Big Bang happen, Who

desired to be known. And this

lizard who's writing all this down late at
night, the galaxies working their boundaryless
way through heaven, situated in shadow,
under his figurative leaf,
plucking from the heavens the succulent firefly of
thought and gulping it down, hoping to

expand past green scaliness, lizard claws,
hoping to catch the Great Glimpse and so be
utterly transformed,

this lizard
is myself.

1/22

SOME SHAFT OF LIGHT

We are all running in place in a
   shaft of God's Light.

I was inspired to this seeing a
young man running at 7A.M. wintry morning
   along the Schuylkill River in
     sweat pants and sweat shirt
flopping his arms, his face so innocent and
open, his mouth slightly open, eyes focused
straight ahead, running forward I guess as I
drove by, and it struck me we're actually

running in place in that shaft, sometimes
elevated, sometimes lifted out of ourselves, some even
raised to permanent levels, in

a shaft of God's perfect Light, not actually
going anywhere, not really
arriving from anywhere, our whole bodies

shaken up and down as if by the
force of our heartbeats, earth-shaken, quaking
mightily in place, faces as
innocent as birds, open to whatever
comes, mouths slightly
open as if to taste something sweet or say words,

some of us becoming suddenly

totally still, lifted
totally out of ourselves and replaced
entirely by God's
Light, that

same exact shaft we formerly were
running in place in, now

expanded from deep
within to way
past us, encompassing things that are
way beyond us,
eyes above seeing level, seeing
sights only few see, then
seeing straight into those who
face us, the
saintly ones whose sight's become
pure meaning,

while we continue to run in place in that single
shaft of God's Light,

fully alive in that running and

fully alive in that Light.

2/1

SOMETHING ABOUT SLEEP

Something so sweet about sleep!
How you pull a pillow under your head
to get comfortable,
rabid buffalo on stampeding rampage from the east,
and curl your body slightly with your
twin knees touching and pulled
up to the chin,
freak fluorescent tidal wave a mile high curls up from the
   bottom of the bedroom wall about to
      crest,
facing to the left with left hand cupping fuzzy head and
tired eyes closing to listen for
angels,
a big bog belches sulfurous vapors that
   seep through the window
extending the skeletal interior out full stretch
and letting the cool interior consciousness
   float from earth to earth —
drought blight famine plague Apocalypse crackdown of
millennial doom at the front door and back—
feeling even the toes relax, the fingers,
all grasping and clutching let go,
all space let go of to flow away where it will.

There's a space in the earth where we'll
sleep a deeper sleep.
A light awaits to awake us.
Fog seeps in filling all the cracks and corners.

Blue mist enters and lays down its
vertical blanket.

There's something so
Sweet about sleep!

2/5

SOME SOFTLY FALLING RAIN

How can we talk about love? It's a
glass tumbler full of flames, coiling up like
    flowing hair, tips
  evaporating in space, then

performing dogs leap barking through flaming
hoops and come out the
other side, tails wagging, and way down

in the interior of a rose, deep and
dark red, those dogs are seen to be
leaping, perfect glistening dew drops
falling inside, each a reflector of

entire oceans and their horizons, skies with three small
clouds scudding across into
total evaporation, with total evaporation of the
sky as well, and of the ocean and air,

until all that's left are deep terrific sonic
booms of the
love that binds the
grasshopper to its food, the
eagle to its heights and the
train to its trestle
high in the Andes where you

look down, if you dare, into mist-filled chasms,

rivers of fog snaking warily through the peaks,
smoky gray and blue with tips of green
trees poking out,

and a starlit night accentuates it, an early
dawn's pale gold trim on the black
uneven horizon accentuates it,

almost spells it out in vaporous letters forming

delicate love words (dog barks in the distance)
spoken from
water to air and back again as

softly falling rain.

2/7

SOME MOMENTS OF EXPANSION

I'm in an all-night restaurant in Iowa called
the "Old Chicago," in a world that's definitely
as irrational-seeming, under a
television screen with sound turned off
where Conan O'Brien is interviewing Stephen King,
hatchet-mouthed and slitty reptile-eyed behind
coke-bottle glasses, and a song on the
jukebox caught my heart with its guitar rhythms
to float out into space with open soul
fluttering forward with all mankind to where
cosmic winds blow our faces and our
bodies dissolve into bands of light

and I can almost read Stephen King's lips as he
gestures with intensely stretched fingers and
turns back and forth in his blue chair,

and it seems the feeling was momentary
and filled with love

pulse pulse billowing goldenness blue through hoops of
space and light out and out
beyond this world singing with sure throat

heart riding high on oceans
of space

SOME THOUGHTS IN THE AIR

This could be a poem with everything in it.
I'm up in an airplane that could fall out of the sky
any minute.
There's land out the window, and silvery water.
The pierced Puerto Rican guy from the R&B group next to me
("The Voices of Theory") has slept the whole flight, head back, hands
   politely folded on a pillow on his lap
with the longest curly black eyelashes I've ever seen
on softly closed lids. Where he's flown I'll
never know, nor maybe he
neither, unless it's simply
Dallas.
Voices surround me, parts of conversations, earnest
replies, fragmented laughter, the great long

voice of mankind ribboning in and out of
immaterial labyrinths, the glancing of
eyes, the shaking of heads. The darting
forward of meaning, probing and dodging questions eliciting
   replies, boasts and
fabrications.

The plane lurches down. My
last will and testament. No god but God.
Blackened patchwork fields below as the
   plane tilts to turn. People

below as well as this

plane full of people going to
join them in their
dark pursuits. My self as

well. Coughing and talking. Sleeping and
keeping silent. The wall of

it all, and the sudden,
miraculous breach.

2/12

SOME MYSTERIOUS TRANSFORMATIONS

1

This could be the end, or it could be the
    beginning. A
rooster in a barnyard suddenly decided he was
worthy of something greater, so he grew
arms and a human head and spoke
slow enraptured sentences that people for
miles around came to listen to.
Not a bad trick for a rooster. Easy for
    God. Though there is some

controversy among scholars regarding the
radical breaking of norms. Yet

the mountain that wanted to be
closer to heaven became a
    sputtering volcano, and the
light that wanted to be perceived by men
broke into rainbow bands visible as
the color spectrum to the naked eye. Now
flowers are red and orange, fields are green and
yellow, clouds are silvery blue and
the depths of the lake are deep purple going into
black. A face so

beautiful it becomes ethereal
floats for a moment like a

bubble above this blank sheet of paper.
Opens its mouth and dictates this poem.

It could be the end or it could be the beginning

but it's always somewhere in the middle,
middle of a song, middle of a sentence,
middle of a life. Both ends like
slowly beating wings, until we

rise up off the ground and tilt
horizontally toward the Light.

2

The camel that drank water from a trough and
    became convinced it was a prime minister,
the cup that touched the lips of a prime minister
and became convinced it was the Holy Grail,
the Holy Grail that lived in mystery and obscurity
convinced no one would find it, until a
    stable boy came upon it
        shining in a woodshed window,
his heart purified by sorrow and his
vision by intense faith. He
    drank from the chalice and became
saintly and unafraid, flew across the city in the
night as luminous as the moon,
and walked from village to village protecting
mistreated animals and

humans without hope. No one ever
    knew his name.

The world revolved like a toy marble at his
fingertips. The world
slipped into his heartbeats unnoticed
and out again as an idle thought.
The world was a reflection on the surface of a
jug of water.
The jug of water was poured into a trough.
A camel drank the water from the
trough and became
convinced he was someone
    very important.
He became convinced he was the prime minister
of a country of luminous beings.
These luminous beings might be ourselves.
It would take another
   luminous being to discover it.
The love of two luminous beings
    lights up the world.
God bestows luminosity
   on whom He will.

3

Sing a song of breath and let the rest go.
Sing a song of light and let the dark go.
Sing a song of windows in a blank wall.
Sing a song of doors where you would want to go.

The garden sings all by itself to passing birds.
Birds carry the garden's song to a solitary singer.

A horn in the night sings the song and then falls silent.
Was it a truck in the distance, or
   Israfil's horn of the Resurrection?

Listen with an ear that enlightens the love that
pervades the air.

Everywhere song is sung suddenly out of nowhere.
We carry the voice of the cosmos within us
light as a feather.

Tickle the throat into song
before we are gone.

The song is sung at the end and beginning of
   each song.

The song I sing of never ends. It is
pure song.

2/14

SOME SIMPLE EXPLANATON

The simplest explanation is a
    flute on the lips, a
butterfly that lands on the tip of a pencil,
black and white spots that turn iridescent as it flies away, a
slowly burning house abandoned in the hills
where no one ever walks any more, and
no one is buried, a bronze glow
    cast on an entire city, reflected in
flat black water, air riffling pages in a book, they
fan in an arc from the fulcrum of the spine, and the
first scattered raindrops hits them and
    beats them down.

The simplest explanation is done before the
moment has completely passed, it's the
shadow of a small gnat cast, for it magnificently,
against a tree twig the size of a super highway
    suspended in space, it's an

infectious smile or a laugh that begins in the
back of a room and travels forward, throat by
throat, to the front. It's also
an astounding hill at high sea, sudden stasis, sudden
ballroom floor glistening in the noon sun,
no one talking all at once, and then suddenly
    noticing, and talking again, the

flick of an eye from glance to glance, the soft

shift of a foot as the weight of a body shifts,
a name spoken so clearly it wakes us up out of a
deep state we didn't even realize was sleep,

heartbeat like a subtle tropical sway, palm tree or stiff
Bird of Paradise flower, bright
orange flare against bright blue sky, as

simple an explanation of the inexplicable as
any other. That sensation that things are actually

heading backwards, slipping rapidly back to an
origin out of time. But with a

face on them. Eyes like planetary space. Lips like
the simple command to the creation: *Be!*

2/17

SOME MISCHANCES

You get close
  and a puddle of
light comes between you. You

slide right in, and you see the whole
set's disappeared, a chair
    left behind, a
hat already on it.

Fences, miles of fences. Some
windblown, some with posters, most
just fences. Right

down to the sea.
Bits of popular song, sung at
appropriate intervals, sometimes the
lyrics meshing perfectly with
what's happening, but most
usually not.

Snakes, red and jet black, slithering,
everywhere, only a
trick of light?

I wish. When they're
gone, they leave snake skins.
Brittle husks.

Hush. The little ones are
trying to sleep. Or actually, just
being. Sleepy. Whereas

cats wake up early for action, it
takes us a long time, then we're
pooped.

I reach out for your hand.
If you take mine, please be
kind. All kinds of

shark infest these waters.
It's too early to think
anything clearly. It's

already too late.

2/19

SOME LATE NIGHT POSITIONING

The vole's asleep in his burrow, and the
   rat and the spider.
The woodpecker's finished with pecking and
   nestles in a hole he's pecked,
the lamb, the fox in his den, the
criminal President of Serbia, tucked in, snoozing,
giraffes in the zoo down the street are
asleep however giraffes manage to sleep,
dolphins in the dark bay are floating midway
   in a sleep that comes up for air,
even flies in their dung heaps have decelerated
and somehow close those multiple eyes for a
nap, peculiar to insects, same with
gnats, taking gnat naps.

Saints are at prayer, standing, sitting or
on their sides, faces concentrated, minds constantly
growing less dark, hearts literally
   flooding with light, their
small rooms lit by a single candle
tilting slightly as if the
rooms want to sleep even if their
   inhabitants don't.

Great masters might be flying. Through the air,
visiting their disciples, ministering to the
sick, mending a ruined life or two with a
touch of light.

And somewhere between the
animals, the criminals and the
lone and isolate holy ones attempting to scale the
unscalable razorback heights
to God, I sit on bed-edge scribbling a
poem nobody might read, whose

little life takes place in the blue-lined
pages of my notebook at 3A.M. on a
Saturday night, another dot of life

turning with the
rapidly turning globe in the dark.

2/21

SOME WORDS TO THE HEART

O heart, longing for wings of fire
to fly through the immaterial
window out to a landscape of vast dimensions
beyond this world

to your Beloved Who set up this world for you
to see through to Him, transparent as

glass, this world the very window you need to
fly through to Him,

each of its obstacles a love letter sent direct to
you from Him,

each of its magnificent banquets a love-gift and a
test that you be satisfied with nothing
but Him,

the dark night, the long dark night, its
cliffs and volcanoes, its ghostly presences, its
diaphanous absences, its distant
piano music, its shouts as if from
another room, its gong resounding as if from the
bottom of a well, its
foundering ship at high sea, its
fog-bound rescue, the one who
comes through the fog to you with smooth
incredible hands, who looks at you with a

gaze only seen in the faces of eagles,

O heart, you're not alone on this earth, and
two nights are not the two walls of your prison,
and two more nights the next two, and day the
ceiling and death the floor, and the
breaths you take the food slid under the door,

and your own face the jailer who taunts you
refusing your freedom, O heart

made by the Heart-Breaker, Whose
healing touch is felt best after a wound,
the mortal wound of our life dealt by the
single blow of our birth, O heart.

Be still, your wings will come
when the world is done.

2/21

SOME POETRY

Some poetry's written with eyes closed.
Some poetry's written with eyes open.

Dining room table with rose-flowered place mats,
refrigerator humming at 2:12A.M., I've
just had a bowl of cereal with milk and a bagel with
cream cheese and halva, my little white
heart pill against heart fibrillation, washed down with
cranberry juice in a deep cobalt blue glass,
sitting in my pants and undershirt,

now my eye's are closed,
green Tahitian sunlight splashes across a black beach,
dreamy brown-skinned people move slowly around,
there's a fruity atmosphere in the air, and
warmth in the nostrils,

now I'm back in the dining room with
58 year old white man's arms and hands, one,
the right one, clutching the pen that pulls black
letters out of nowhere onto this page, like
drawing spider thread out of a spider's behind,
writing flowing as I move my hand across to the right like a
typewriter carriage,

now my eyes are closed and I'm in a
Russian circus, black tights with sequins on the
performers as they hop onto cantering

horses in the ring and leap
off again, sometimes bounding across the
   ring onto a loping horse with
      astonishing precision, to have
spent their lives perfecting this superfluous art!
Even getting killed or permanently
damaged in the process, if they
      miss the passing horse, into a
hearse, the entire circus walking in full
costume behind, the circus orchestra playing with
cymbals and glockenspiels, carrying the failed
acrobat to his rest,

now it's night again in Philadelphia,

you want to shake the universe open
once and for all, let all the light out, shining on
everyone at once. William Bronk is dead.
Ginsberg's dead. Olson's dead, Robert Duncan,
the yakkety mouthpieces are
moving spectrally in the
world beyond this one, testing their

theories and perceptions against the

Absolute.

2/26

SOME ABYSS OF LIGHT

The most brightly colored toucan in a tree
can't encapsulate this world's beauty entirely,

nor the choppiest waves at high sea
encase the terrors of the deep in deadliest tragedy,

nor light on lake water late at night, starlight,
create a scintillant otherworldly reality,

that even comes close to the awesomeness it is,
the beauty and terror of it, flash of light

full against the face, facing an abyss of light so
vast one's fear is it'll encompass and engorge us utterly.

2/27

SOME RECOLLECTIONS

I remember the day the dawn came up like a flower
you put in your lapel. And you

did and sauntered away.
And the buildings let you enter them
because they were unafraid, and the

ninety-nine harps leaning against the walls
sounded from their lowest strings to their
    highest when you passed.

I remember the town square in that foreign country that was
to you more welcoming than your own,
children in short red pants and bright green shirts,
    carrying banners with, to us,
indecipherable slogans in an incomprehensible
alphabet we presumed they were
    chanting over and over below them
as they marched twenty abreast and blocked off the
street thronged with all the people of the town,
old women in black, young women in
flowery skirts, dark eyed men looking
    preoccupied with the
innermost equations of an impossible love.

Do you remember the words you said to me
through the stems of the purple chenille flowers
you held up to your face like a veil?

They lit up my months and cast a
glow around my body as I walked. For I am an

adherent to the power of speech, and live in its
spectral fortress on the side of a hill
where the rain of love continually washes down its streets.

Those of us who've left have always
encountered you, and it is your
soul that talks of fear in terms of bravery,
that talks of wounds in terms of healing,
that talks of idiosyncrasy in terms of compassion,
that talks of love in terms of the
flame-intoxicated butterfly whose
wings are transparent by day, but whose
wings turn black as night by
night

it flutters down unknown corridors in search of
the source of that harp sound, and it is
your soul that opens to us like the doors of
glass elevators in buildings of sky towers!

I've been to the place where beauty is architecturally plotted,
where it is molded into shapes and sent to
market, but it pales in comparison with
one glance from your eyes direct into mine.

One glance enough to last
a lifetime.

2/28

SOME MORNING

I wake up without a sound.
I lift my head from the pillow and look around.
The poplar tree is over there instead of
   over there. The bureau's become a

burro patiently standing and chewing and
waiting for me. Waiting for me for what?
To take me away from here to there? Where is

there anyway? I sense a menagerie.
A toucan flies from tree to tree, astonishingly
long beak out front that looks like it would
unbalance the bird, but it's a

fruit eater and the beak is light as paper.
I close my aching eyes. A silver place.

Wonder where the unicorn lives. All this before
standing up full height on earth, another
moment added to my life, another
chopped off the path from now to death,
little black shop at the end of the road where
very innocent animals also stand chewing, and a
sudden quiet descends, a pure
passing of time, time taking place

inside our skin and bones, the old
death thing, a crazed skipper coming for us on a

boat over dry land, doesn't matter,
cutting right into fields and houses and
important events and future circumstances,
every relationship long-lasting or just beginning,

right smack up to us wherever we are, Charon,
blowing the ferry horn, blasting through every
sound possible, even volcanic eruption, even
deadly calm.

So I stand up, take a step forward,
and look around.

Throw water on my face,
wash elbows and feet.

Put my head on the ground.

3/1

SOME VISION OF PRAYER

To pray is to throw pebbles into a lake
in the high Alps, short tundra grass all around,
bright gray sky, the only sound
the tiny plips of stone into water.

To pray is to talk out of oneself, to
   talk oneself out of the single
sovereignty of the self, not just
breath left on a mirror, kissing
   our own lips on the mist,

but calling out across a horse-galloping
   valley as in Mongolia, a
remote place where the
cry reverberates among hardy fir trees and
    continues to resound, softer and
softer down descending valleys to the

smoke-twirling village below where an
old man chops wood while a
girl-baby gazes in wonder from the
back of her mother. A silence that, in itself,
has tone and timbre. That
spreads between the trees and
mountains like a cloth, caressing each
green needle, each creature looking with
eyes and smelling with nostrils.

To pray is to ascend beyond gravity
while remaining very low, lower than
    before, and
spreading oneself out while
centralizing one's heartbeat, the heart thinking,
sinking into its darkness like a miner,
emerging in a place of greater
openness, where other

living souls congregate, bathed in prayer's
splendor, where even the murmurings of the
dead may be heard

among high cracking branches and the
moist rustling of worms underground.

                                                    3/2

SOME SAND GRAINS

"Magnificent!" is the only way to describe it.
How about *"opulent!"*

That one grain of sand?
"Luxuriant." A paragon among sand grains.

But nestled with its kin becomes
 anonymous.

*"Never loses its gemlike splendor. Shines
in God's eyes from whatever distance."* Is a

staircase to heaven for some creature, nor

do I exaggerate.
As if from a precious necklace from which
the string's been removed. She

stepped from her carriage and her
umbrella tip caught in it and it
snapped, and all the jewels scattered, and

that's what desert and beaches have become, sun-baked and
bleached forever, her

scattered darlings, beads all the way to the horizon.

Pick one up and its perfect color dazzles, its

perfect shape anatomizes. I see inside

the universe reversed. Outside of it
projected far and wide. One sand grain

pure magnificence.
Rests in wonder.

Never ceases to amaze.
Encapsules thunder.

3/4

SOME STORY

1

One day the tiniest creature you ever saw
met the hugest creature in all creation
and because opposites attract, they
   got along beautifully. Very

careful with each other, the tiny creature would
nestle in the giant's thick fur, the giant would
lower his voice to speak to her. Pretty soon

they couldn't stand to be away from each other, or
even think about anything or anyone else. They

became each other's space. When their
eyes blinked open in the morning, as they
registered reality and thanked
God for another day alive, the thought of each
other snapped into place like a
fact of nature. Sounds like

true love. Well, a
war broke out. Soldiers
marched into battle. All available
manpower was required to fight. The
giant was drafted. He
had to stay naked since no
uniform could fit him, but his

fur kept him modest, and inside his fur

that tiny creature hid so she could
sing to him in the midst of battle, so his
long nights wouldn't be
lonely, so she
wouldn't hear bad news of him from
far away.

2

The matchbox slid out of reach, the horses
stood in the mud, the night
pulled down like a tent. Flares
lit up a dark hill. The faces of youths were
illumined by death, their thoughts worn down by
life. Cups of hot broth were brought to their
lips in their cots with blood-clots and
spume from hurt bodies strewn around in the
disarray and hurry of war. The giant

spoke in whispers to his beloved. He talked of
islands, cakes, bicycles, flight. They would
live forever on an island eating cakes, riding
bicycles. She listened and stroked his breast.
She spoke in perfect sentences. Her love was
resilient to pain. They would
endure.

3

They endured. Was it in
   this world or the next? Red suns, blue
      clouds, gorgeous water,
green grass tall as trees, trees in full flower,
as if covered with bells. Lights of all
colors and shapes floated freely in the
air, bent and slowly
twisted like syntax, unfurling like a
phrase pursuing its
meaning to the end. And the end included

enchantment, silvery-edged waves and a
surf so soft eggs could be laid in it and
rocked gently without harm. Hatched into
flying birds. And the giant lay, not

asleep and not awake, and his
tiny lover also
neither asleep nor awake
danced in front of his eyes and sang

songs into first one ear than the other
as the sun sank down and
rose again before they noticed.

Summer and winter came without hindrance.
Tidal waves threatened, the sky lowered to the
tips of their eyelids and lifted. They were

unafraid. They moved now with a
deeper movement. The war had slipped

inside their bones where it now played
flute music. Flares no longer
visited their eyes. Only lakes, lagoons,
trees as if floating in air,

sweet aromas dusting their pollen
everywhere.

                                                      3/5

SOME COORDINATES

Where are we on the planet, exact coordinates,
hairline sight that locates us exactly at
   any given time, walking lazily along,
running in our twinkly shoes, those

absolute longitudinal and latitudinal wire-mesh
lines of location, the physical body with its
hair follicles and sweat glands crossing this

earth on foot, going under a bridge, ambling
next to a fast-rushing river, or two of us, two
needing those coordinates that would

project out into space and be some extremely
technical kind of algebra, especially as
one of them leans toward the
other and takes the other's hand, or even
presses his lips against the other's cheek or neck

at exactly a point which can be plotted and
circumscribed and through which
migrating Canada geese happily honking at each
other high up in the sky fly on their way to the Keys,
while below the couple's been
increased by two more who've met them on the
path and are mildly marveling at the
small world that actually put them together at
exactly this time and place when it is

extremely miraculous that anyone cross each other's
path on their way to or from anywhere, the
microbes and bacterium as well, noodling along on

a path or many forking and bifurcating
paths from the silver lake of creational light to
the silver lake of annihilation, exhilarating

as it is, in between the two,
to behold!

3/8

SOMETHING

Something lit up the sky. Or
was it Your Face?
Something wore the jewels of the stars of the sky
as a crown.
Something shook under our
   feet. Was it the heartbeat
that pulsates the world into being?
We walk obliviously most of the time, our hearts

somewhere as if in a glass case beating alone
full of wishes. I wish I were a

fish in the Azores or swimming in turquoise
waters around the Greek Isles, or I wish

love would flatten me completely, would run totally
roughshod over every last vestige of
doubt and self-safety, so I might,

you know, expand past the sea's horizon and keep
going toward Your Face above the waters You've so
expertly created for us to swim in. Ah

God, how You let us speak on such intimate
terms with You, Creator of massive boulders and fathoms
deep in the sea, of Mars and Jupiter and

Neptune wreathed in clouds, of lips so perfectly

kissable and words like these, our
blood pulsing in our wrists and the rapid running of
deer or the disappearance of rabbits into the
background so you can't
see them at all at dusk munching
grass by the bushes, freezing still.

We are at rest and full of anger. Nothing is going quite
right for us. This is a letter of complaint. But I'm

complaining to the Creator of Roman legions and terrorists, of
serial murderers and nurses, of rebellious upheavals and
mud slides that cover
entire Venezuelan villages, I'm
raising this tiny mouse voice above that roar!

How many blows do we receive in this life, Lord,
until we're

as useless as sand in a high wind?

(I won't speak until I'm spoken to.)

3/10

SOME TRICK

The trick is maybe to write a poem that never stops,
that gathers speed especially when going uphill,
that attaches to itself the various
   paraphernalia of death as well as
spring blossoms, exotic beetles, especially those
green iridescent ones, seal whiskers, love letters from both
nearby and far away, both to and
from the Beloved, salted slightly and tied with
sweet umbilical ribbon,

the trick is maybe to have an unending vision
unrolling from right to left and from
left to right simultaneously of whatever
comes to birth in a split second and then takes
its destined time to die, of magenta as it splashes against black,
of a deeper black than anyone's ever imagined,
squares and tall rectangles and wide
horizontals of black going infinitely back and
back into a background that
also gives way to a yet
deeper shade of black,

the music of such blackness,
unimaginable chords that evoke blackness
which is finally at the uttermost
limit of black and is the actual source of
our heart's ability to see light,

the trick is maybe to never give up hope while still
maintaining that level-headed realism the human
animal is so lauded for
though not by the other animals,
to put our best and only face forward, our
eyes stinging from salt spray,
to comb our hair with our fingers
and say Yes with the encircling of our hands
around what can't be encircled and yet is
contained in the momentary gesture of
palms and fingers peacefully weaving the air,

the trick is of course to have no trick,
the hourglass already tipped and the
Sahara almost entirely gone through the pinhole,
wrinkles appear like lightning forks on the
   backs of our hands,
memory acts like an old car in the snow,
turns over a few times but takes a long time to catch,
a long time to ignite into action,

memory needs to shatter like a wall of icicles
before the flame of the perfect moment,
our appreciation of their pearl-like rotundity and
diamond-like glitter,
each on a string moving forward through our
fingers like an oxygen rosary,

the trick is to blast apart the frozen doors of our being
to a hillside of illumined

deer each perfectly poised, each nose tilted with
utmost sensitivity, awaiting our
slightest movement to trigger them all
bounding away like star-rays,

to walk through the body-shaped walls of our own
resistance to what is actually already with us,

already aglow like a dim planet
    swimming into view
from our lunar horizon hovering above ourselves,

barren but shining.

3/12

SOME ARTIFACTS

First the fishes then the loaves, the
rigging and bowsprit of the ark, the hold with its
multiple stalls, hay-carpeted, branches of

the forbidden tree, the Y's of their
   heavily freighted forks,
the moneychangers' tables, legs broken off from
     being smashed, none of the
coins themselves unfortunately, the
tables actually pretty much in splinters, splinters
from the true cross, from Abraham's hacked and fallen idol, from
the coffin Lazarus lay in and rose from the first time,
wood from the Ark of the Covenant, from the

staff of Moses he held aloft to part the sea,
splinters from that staff, the one he

threw before the astonished Egyptian magicians, now not
serpent-like but bent and
twisted and actually pretty much in splinters as well, all these

holy artifacts, nothing in themselves except the
role they played, Stanley Kowalski's ripped T-shirt,
the guillotine blade that sliced
Louis XVI's head clean off its royal body
and kept slicing through the cold cuts of social inequality,
slice slice right down snicker-snack the flashing blade
each molecule of these artifacts aglow since everything's

aglow that takes place in this life, and in the

story bigger than life itself that continues to
animate its glory, runs underneath every
plot we can devise and every so often
bursts full-bodied to the surface,

the olive branch brought back by that bird
signifying land, there in the
glass case clearly marked with the
dramatic spotlight trained down on it
as it sits on black velvet
retired from active service, collecting
residuals from just having ever been at all
for even just a single moment
figuring prominently in the human drama.

Footprints on the rock where
Abraham stood supervising the Ka'ba, footprints in the

African desert where one of our black ancestors passed
imprinting the earth ever so lightly,

the bell of that one
print still ringing. Its tree still

pushing out buds.

3/13

SOME MATTER

All the matter in this universe can be condensed into a
spot of light on the side of a vase full of

long stemmed red roses covered in bluish mist
bouncing along a cobble-stoned street in the back of a
wooden cart painted with scenes from the village below
up a hill to a threading network of roads each with
the same cart drawn by the same horse
with the same vase with an identical
gleam of light shining on it

or into a spot of light within that light,

all the matter of the universe condensed
and able somehow to emerge intact again,
this wire-mesh round-cornered hard-edged
profile and full-face universe going through its
    paces at twenty paces on a
foggy morning and suddenly there's a
spot of light on the pistol of one of the duelists
and all the matter of the universe can just as
easily be condensed into that spot,

the counting off by the second, he takes his
    time between each additional number,
there's a silence then a shot,
one goes down but manages to fire a
shot in the now blurry general direction of his

opponent covered in blood,

the whole universe in that momentary spot of
   light that preceded this
     patch of darkness actually
covering them both now with the unfurled
instantaneous cape of their deaths,

or in the eye of the sparrow hawk that just
happened to fly by at that very moment on its
early morning rounds, dawn's new light casting a
spot in its eye wheeling into the trees,
the whole universe of matter condensed also into that
spot, so much intelligence in that
     gaze,

or into that spot of light on your perfect
teeth when you smile,

the whole universe of matter in that spot
just in time to be

    sealed by a kiss.

3/17

SOME DETAILS

Little tiny flourishes, something in the
   margins of all that exists,
feathery writing sideways, slanting at an
   angle from sunlight or Night Blooming
Cereus in forest depths, deep booms of
heartbeat or bass beat in
sea depths, passing of flatfish past each other's
flatness in pitch dark waters,
rice floating in air,
brass jugs ascending slowly in space, pouring out their
   contents over entire continents,
liquidesque iridescent corkscrews catching sunlight,
splendid curlicues enveloping everything,
illuminated String Theory, tiny wriggling threads connecting
horse races to star shine, bus brakes to
nuns at prayer, I

squint through space, loops of rainbow twilight,
wrinkles in the main emanation, time stands
still at a pin drop, the room I'm in stands still
while fish swim, adorable
   smile, lips fit for kissing, I'm
so lost without You, tendrils leading from
twisting flame tips, traveling up vines to the flat-topped
mountaintop, we gaze down at the
ocean, we roll on our sides and see green
surf roll, seabirds wheeling and

diving, blue
waves rolling over them.

3/20

SOME LAST WISHES

When I die, hammer my sliver back into the
    main wood,
paint my blue into the back of the blue chair,
file my rough down into basic smooth
   (though I should have done that
      while alive),

I shall chart these waters no longer, go up these
    dead end tributaries for no one but
my own self's living wonderment, as if

anything we do has buttons and special snaps on it
for anyone but ultimately ourselves, though that
should encompass moon and stars, the
echo long after speech heard later by all the
gentle woodland creatures, all the
violent Darwinian beasts battling it out by that
same moonlight, antler to antler and
horn to horn, the crack of collision heard throughout the
terrible valleys, resounding among the
    horrible hills —

when I die let these sky-gazing eyes float
freely back into the sky in which they were born
and let their gaze never avert from anyone but You,
   heart and soul
fringed by eyelashes, watching the
   frail boats of my final heartbeats

set sail in their pure black waters,

both clear and perfectly still.

4/3

SOME FLUTE MUSIC

1

I would write a poem so sad
birds fall out of the trees. But that's

ridiculous, and what birds would sit still for such a
sad poem? The lament of the lone

flute player by the side of the Nile, OK, the
orphan flute player who's hungry and alone, who
never knew his father or mother, who was made to
sweep a courtyard all his childhood and gather
firewood all his youth, who's really ugly and
half blind, barefoot, scrawny and unloved, but who
plays the flute so beautifully and with such
tender feeling that birds actually don't fall
out of trees but flock to the tree branch
closest to the boy in order to hear new
tunes by a soul so deep and a heart so full only
birds really understand the unspeakable

truth of his song. The story could continue, but

trucks go by and college students with
ghetto blasters, and a barge horn sounds so that
the flute melody through which actual
gnats fly in symmetrical formations is nearly
   drowned out completely

by the insensitivities of the actual world around
him and around us as well, and his

deep sadness feeds the intervals of the notes he plays,
and they have this heart-tugging effect, the melodic leaps are
unexpected and both mournful and ecstatic,
lamenting the dangers and grief at a
cold-hearted world as well as the unreasonable
joy and hope in the little
things that seem to fall to us off a shelf of such
knickknacks in heaven as well as the somehow
immense ocean of trust in God that washes inexplicably
around the human heart even in the face of horrors.

2

A cat's life is adequate to a cat.
A gnat's life is adequate to a gnat.
Is a cat sad he can't look up at us and just say
"Please pass the mouse?"

Is the gnat troubled or preoccupied,
does it go into an empty jar and buzz around erratically because
it's suffering unrequited love?

Everything seems to go along in its pattern, weaving and
unweaving itself into and out of the major
ongoing design, the star design, the
autonomous orbit, the
mask of the invisible, ribbons in space,
ripples across an ocean-size drop of water that actually
fits into the hollow of a spoon.

Our sad histrionics, which make us all too human,
which look best if we're holding a
broom or cleaning the cat box, the
    Narcissus helmet that
      comes around our head with its
multiple mirrors like bad Feng Shui, the
warble of our inner voice unable to
      sustain High-C for long before breaking,

while somewhere a real tear is shed by someone in real pain

and out of that tear bursts the world.

3

Oh I know the sound of the flute is a
    sad and mournful sound,
coming through the long brass tubes of the ears
to way inside the mind, under its
    sunny dome, watching for strangers
who might lead us out of this gloom, a new
moon-like face to reflect our sad face in,

that lone boy on the Nile with the
triangular-sailed feluccas gliding by on grease wavelets,
    (is the Nile a deep jade green?
    A rhinoceros-hide blue-gray?)
and how the notes from his flute are
suspended long enough to become a flock of

      ibises in flight, a convoy of
ancient extraterrestrials, small and darting,
the skyline of jumbled Cairo buildings before
    vaporizing back into a sound that
hovers in the air, then falls as a thin spray on
anyone walking near. He's

looking into the air and seeing all this, as if he were
the rich man only a few hundred yards away in his villa
searching in his closet for a fresh galabeyya.
His closet is the lively nowhere that is
God's breathing space all around him as he

gets up from his concert (taking a bow or two from the
flapping duck ovation) and sticking his flute in his
back pocket flops slope-shouldered home.
Out of his terrible loneliness (etcetera), his

sweet music gilding the low-flying clouds, his
momentary spotlight in broad daylight on the
riverbank of a patch of photorealism,
fingers working reed holes gingerly,

eyes so black night checks itself in them
the way a woman checks her makeup before
going out. Night learns its darkness from the

flute player's eyes, then spreads it out
into the air.

                                            4/4-9

SOME SHOPS

I have seen some little shops where
   broken things are sold
and the shops are always full of eager customers.
There's a set of matches that won't light,
unreadable books because their
   pages are blank, plans for a
lost city, love letters on ice.
The "almost-new" kit of Torture & Death, Displacement &
Hate isn't actually broken and
sells for a song. Many buyers seem to be
  going out the door with it under their
     arms.

I've seen shops that sell birdseed for sparrows,
Chinese newspapers, kites.
The proprietor is so small he has to
stand on your hand to be heard.

I've gone into the store that sells visions,
the salesman is overly happy, the walls
   disappear, there always seem to be
more horses than could conceivably
fit in such a small space, and some are
   flying.

But the shop at the end of the street, the one
unfrequented, where they sell what
can't be expressed or priced, whose

trade value can't be measured by any market category,
where only a few people go, one at a time,
who come out with nothing visibly added to them,
empty-handed, but utterly different and
strange, who from then on avoid shopping,
who speak in short musical sentences,
whose eyes exhilarate anyone who gazes into them
    even for the fraction of a second,

the shop with its own sunlight pouring
    down on it, its own
moonlight, and whose

proprietor is hidden and manifest both, but

never visible…

4/11

SOME NEW DIMENSIONS

At the limits of this universe, at the tips of all its little
   pinpoints, begins another one

with all its up stairways going down and all its
down stairways going up, black roses twined on all the
   balustrades exuding honey, bright round
     moon faces smiling at all the windows.
I open a love letter and blue
steam writes the contents in giant swirls in the air,

bridges fly unattached over green waters,
willow trees like women's hair
spreading undulant tresses over green waves.

The new universe extends itself out from the burnt shell of this one
stretched to its limits, and

everything in the new one flows so charmingly
until you begin to see that everything
flows as charmingly in this one too,
a body doesn't move through the
same air twice even if it remains motionless,
   or if it actually

gets up and moves, the whole universe of air and
dimension changes all around it,

with no way to tell which is moving, which is not.

Long shadows extend over a rippling lake.

Everything moves along so normally you
begin to wonder if you've made the whole thing up.

This universe contains it all.
The wider universe is actually contained
perfectly in this one.

Open a shell and out it blooms.
Put a seed in the ground and a
    tree rises.

4/13

SOME RANDOM NOTES

1

Somnambulists under the sea have become
    impatient to fall asleep.
Church bells ring but it doesn't hinder the
    mating calls of the elephant.
It's a very red sunset, here on the deck of the
    Titanic, *blood red!*

Everywhere in the world a termite chews, a dragonfly
    darts (well, perhaps not in the
Arctic regions, *confound these generalizations!*)
A poem whose swiftness threatens to swallow itself
whole before it emerges.
Tiny tiles juxtaposed perfectly on a tabletop
    before you. Star shapes, patterns
astronomical, geometrical.

The world is moving all around me, there's a
    small ringing in my ears, I wonder if there's
any point continuing this exercise, my
pen is dutifully writing away, my intellect is
in Java cutting down rubber trees, my
heart, sausage full of holes, cathedral in a
clearing, memory-box,
stepladder to heaven, heart knockwurst, beats.

Knock knock.

No one's there.

Is it day?

2

There's a plainness then a fanciness,
there's tragedy then someone snickers,
there's lights out without warning, then they
   come on like a police lineup, you
      blink and look
     washed out and ill-at-ease.
There's fortuitous meetings, *ah those*
   fortuitous meetings! Especially if you believe
explicitly and implicitly in fate and God's
Eternal Decree. So that
   nothing's left to chance in an
infinite series of rapid scene-changes and
dialog shifts, like playing cards fanning by, only it's
the universe and your life,

illustrations in a book whose page is turned to and the
illustrations on that page, the color one of the
   cloud-capped mountain peak, the elevation
diagram next to it with silhouettes of tall
human creations like the Eiffel Tower
showing the more awesome height of the mountain, plus
photos of some of its wild flowers and a
grinning native holding the clove plant that
grows at its base.

While the book is open to that page, pre-ordained by
being in the book at all, but a
surprise by being the one turned to,
those illustrations come into play, events

clang and fall across our lives, some punks are
snatched away, some are sent to
scare us, mother's voice is heard from the
central room from this world or the next, a tax is
levied on our breaths for our existence, we're

never grateful enough, that's for
certain, we're alive in full
to partial consciousness of that fact, but even if
bubbling in pure ecstasy we're not really
showing God the gratitude He deserves, even though our
both feet be caught in bear traps
and our face in a state of shock
that anything should prevent us from
meeting the Inevitable.

3

The little dolls on the windowsill
   sway to the music
but no one cares. No one sees them
   in the dark.
The white horse outside the window
hides its wings against its flanks and chomps the
   meadow grass as

    nonchalantly as possible.
I wouldn't upset the applecart. No
      shouting allowed.
Drum taps in the distance announce the
  arrival of the militia. But they're

all under twelve and have wings as well.
The whole world's become transparent, translucent
  as glass. You can see

clear through to the other side. And
everything's singing. Raising its golden
voice in the general choir. I wouldn't want to sing a

bass note in such a congregation. Let the
stones and low bridges over rustling waters
do that. The sunbeams with their

high tenors, the trees with their rich baritone harmonies.
The winds hold high-C and some even higher neighboring
notes, some too high even for the
human ear to hear.

The mountainside curls peacefully asleep.
The dead charmer
walks among the living but has no
negative hold on them. He just gazes out from under those
heavy gray lids at the gaiety around him, steady as a

stone falling through water.

I've seen the looks on the faces of those who
recognize him for what he is, and the
looks of those who don't. You could
drive herds of elephants through the difference
between the two. The ones who

recognize him have a wary burnish to the
light in their eyes. They cherish each breath they take.
The others are oblivious, childlike in their
oblivion. Annoyingly high-spirited the way a
cat insists on attention in the middle of an important
sentence when it's already hard enough to
concentrate on the desired outcome.

The militia's armed, waiting, outside the
door. They each have trumpets and bayonets.

They lift the trumpets to their lips and blow.

The world becomes opaque again, and their
bayonets gleam. But the

singing goes on.

4/17-21

SOME OPALESCENT GLEAMS

In the shadow of the temple
   a bright opal gleams,
its rays actually extending in lateral
   bands,
dust motes falling through in the
   cool ancient air.

A stork flapping down beside it and
taking it in its bill then
rising into the air with opal clenched still
shining,
stork wings floating between dust-colored pillars
as it flies out through the broken colonnade into
bright egg-blue sky
skimming the river.

This is a ritual so ancient no one knows its origin.

Stork across the city
glides into another temple opening where a
pair of statue upraised hands awaits to
receive the opal stork drops into them then
stands and folds its wings back into its body and blinks

as the bright opal gleams
in the shadow of the temple.

                                                            4/22

SOME GREAT SOULS HAVE PASSED BY

Some great souls have passed by, leaving, you know,
things written on napkins, armies
   equipped to the teeth for mass destruction,
vaccines against mortal diseases, tomes inches
thick in iambic pentameter, concertos for
shortness of breath and length of endurance.

The culture is an outdoor café where people wave
   multicolored flags each with a slogan.
This poem is a critique against
   I don't know what exactly, trying to
put in their place a few unruly elements of
   existence, as
whole cupboard shelves of homemade jam grow fuzzy purple and
green mold, as house shingles
   fall singly from roofs bearing squirrels who were
minding their own business, twitching
   noses and tails.

People in individual rooms on earth are assiduously
trying to make their mark
or pass through as unnoticed as possible, sometimes
both simultaneously, but

nothing comes automatically or even easily in this
world except to acknowledge the Source with each
   breath whose nimbus we are

rolling along like billiard balls across green felt
and dropping heavily into net pockets from
   time to time, the stick reaching
illuminatedly lengthwise into our often inaccessible corners

to flush us out into the open under His

Ever Compassionate Gaze.

4/25

INDEX

Something About Sleep   89
Some Abyss of Light   110
Some Artifacts   130
Some Attempts at Intimidation   53
Some Coordinates   123
Some Cries   44
Some Cries from the Heart   15
Someday   13
Some Days   22
Some Deaths   14
Some Definitions of Love   61
Some Demon Detractors   82
Some Details   134
Some First Light   11
Some Flashlight Beams   63
Some Flute Music   137
Some Flutterings   71
Some Glimpses of the Dancer   60
Some Good Advice Thrown Out   9
Some Great Souls Have Passed By   151
Some High Ringing Sounds   69
Some Incomprehensible Words   40
Some Indications   17
Some Insectivore Transformations   84
Some Instructions   48
Some Last Wishes   135
Some Late Night Positioning   104
Some Leaves Fall   12
Some Love Thoughts   72
Some Matter   132
Some Minor Miracles   50
Some Mischances   102
Some Moments of Expansion   93

Some Morning   113
Some Mournful Notes   65
Some Mysterious Transformations   96
Some New Dimensions   143
Some Observations   19
Some Opalescent Gleams   150
Some People   21
Some Poetry   108
Some Prayers   29
Some Proof   46
Some Purposes   56
Some Random Notes   145
Some Recollections   111
Some Sad Sounds   35
Some Sand Grains   117
Some Serious Advice   79
Some Shaft of Light   87
Some Shops   141
Some Sights   37
Some Simple Explanaton   100
Some Softly Falling Rain   91
Some Solutions to What's Insoluble   58
Some Steps   33
Some Story   119
Some Tears   31
Something   125
Some Things Left Unsaid   38
Some Thoughts in the Air   94
Some Trees   26
Some Trick   127
Some Vision   42
Some Vision of Prayer   115
Some Words of Reassurance   24
Some Words to the Heart   106

ABOUT THE AUTHOR

Born in 1940 in Oakland, California, Daniel Abdal-Hayy Moore had his first book of poems, *Dawn Visions*, published by Lawrence Ferlinghetti of City Lights Books, San Francisco, in 1964, and the second in 1972, *Burnt Heart/Ode to the War Dead*. He created and directed *The Floating Lotus Magic Opera Company* in Berkeley, California in the late 60s, and presented two major productions, *The Walls Are Running Blood*, and *Bliss Apocalypse*. He became a Sufi Muslim in 1970, performed the Hajj in 1972, and lived and traveled throughout Morocco, Spain, Algeria and Nigeria, landing in California and publishing *The Desert is the Only Way Out*, and *Chronicles of Akhira* in the early 80s (Zilzal Press). Residing in Philadelphia since 1990, in 1996 he published *The Ramadan Sonnets* (Jusoor/City Lights), and in 2002, *The Blind Beekeeper* (Jusoor/Syracuse University Press). He has been the major editor for a number of works, including *The Burdah* of Shaykh Busiri, translated by Hamza Yusuf, and the poetry of Palestinian poet, Mahmoud Darwish, translated by Munir Akash. He is also widely published on the worldwide web: *The American Muslim*, *DeenPort*, and his own website and poetry blog, among others: *www.danielmoorepoetry.com*, *www.ecstaticxchange.wordpress.com*. He has been poetry editor for *Seasons Journal, Islamica Magazine*, a 2010 translation by Munir Akash of *State of Siege*, by Mahmoud Darwish (Syracuse University Press), and *The Prayer of the Oppressed*, by Imam Muhammad Nasir al-Dar'i, translated by Hamza Yusuf. In 2011, 2012 and 2014 he was a winner of the Nazim Hikmet Prize for Poetry. In 2013 he won an American Book Award, and was listed among The 500 Most Influential Muslims for his poetry. *The Ecstatic Exchange Series* is bringing out the extensive body of his works of poetry (a complete list of published works on page 2).

POETIC WORKS by Daniel Abdal-Hayy Moore
Published and Unpublished

Dawn Visions (published by City Lights, 1964)
Burnt Heart/Ode to the War Dead (published by City Lights, 1972)
This Body of Black Light Gone Through the Diamond (printed by Fred Stone, Cambridge, Mass, 1965)
On The Streets at Night Alone (1965?)
All Hail the Surgical Lamp (1967)
States of Amazement (1970)

Abdallah Jones and the Disappearing-Dust Caper (published by The Ecstatic Exchange/Crescent Series, 2006)
'Ala ud-Deen and the Magic Lamp (published by The Ecstatic Exchange, 2011)
The Chronicles of Akhira (1981) (published by Zilzal Press with Typoglyphs by Karl Kempton, 1986; published in Sparrow on the Prophet's Tomb by The Ecstatic Exchange, 2009)
Mouloud (1984) (A Zilzal Press chapbook, 1995; published in Sparrow on the Prophet's Tomb by The Ecstatic Exchange, 2009)
The Crown of Creation (1984) (published by The Ecstatic Exchange, 2012)
The Look of the Lion (The Parabolas of Sight) (1984)
The Desert is the Only Way Out (completed 4/21/84) (Zilzal Press chapbook, 1985)
Atomic Dance (1984) (am here books, 1988)
Outlandish Tales (1984)
Awake as Never Before (12/26/84) (Zilzal Press chapbook, 1993)
Glorious Intervals (1/1/85) (Zilzal Press chapbook, ?)
Long Days on Earth/Book I (1/28 – 8/30/85)
Long Days on Earth/Book II (Hayy Ibn Yaqzan)
Long Days on Earth/Book III (1/22/86)
Long Days on Earth/Book IV (1986)
The Ramadan Sonnets (Long Days on Earth/Book V) (5/9 – 6/11/86) (published by Jusoor/City Lights Books, 1996) (republished as Ramadan Sonnets by The Ecstatic Exchange, 2005)
Long Days on Earth/Book VI (6-8/30/86)
Holograms (9/4/86 – 3/26/87)
History of the World (The Epic of Man's Survival) (4/7 – 6/18/87)
Exploratory Odes (6/25 – 10/18/87)

The Man at the End of the World (11/11 – 12/10/87)
The Perfect Orchestra (3/30 – 7/25/88)(published by The Ecstatic Exchange, 2009)
Fed from Underground Springs (7/30 – 11/23/88)
Ideas of the Heart (11/27/88 – 5/5/89)
New Poems (scattered poems, out of series, from 3/24 – 8/9/89)
Facing Mecca (5/16 – 11/11/89)
A Maddening Disregard for the Passage of Time (11/17/89 – 5/20/90) (published by The Ecstatic Exchange, 2009)
The Heart Falls in Love with Visions of Perfection (6/15/90 – 6/2/91)
Like When You Wave at a Train and the Train Hoots Back at You (Farid's Book) (6/11 – 7/26/91) (published by The Ecstatic Exchange, 2008)
Orpheus Meets Morpheus (8/1/91– 3/14/92)
The Puzzle (3/21/92 – 8/17/93)(published by The Ecstatic Exchange, 2011)
The Greater Vehicle (10/17/93 – 4/30/94)
A Hundred Little 3-D Pictures (5/14/94 – 9/11/95) (published by The Estatic Exchange, 2013)
The Angel Broadcast (9/29 – 12/17/95)
Mecca/Medina Time-Warp (12/19/95 – 1/6/96) (published as a Zilzal Press chapbook, 1996)(published in Sparrow on the Prophet's Tomb, 2009)
Miracle Songs for the Millennium (1/20 – 10/16/96)(published by The Ecstatic Exchange, 2014)
The Blind Beekeeper (11/15/96 – 5/30/97) (published 2002 by Jusoor/Syracuse University Press)
Chants for the Beauty Feast (6/3 – 10/28/97)(published by The Ecstatic Exchange, 2011
You Open a Door and it's a Starry Night (10/29/97 – 5/23/98) (published by The Ecstatic Exchange, 2009)
Salt Prayers (5/29 – 10/24/98) (published by The Ecstatic Exchange, 2005)
Some (10/25/98 – 4/25/99) (published by The Ecstatic Exchange, 2014)
Flight to Egypt (5/1 – 5/16/99)
I Imagine a Lion (5/21 – 11/15/99) (published by The Ecstatic Exchange, 2006)
Millennial Prognostications (11/25/99 – 2/2/2000) (published by the Ecstatic Exchange, 2009)
Shaking the Quicksilver Pool (2/4 – 10/8/2000) (published by The Ecstatic Exchange, 2009)
Blood Songs (10/9/2000 – 4/3/2001)(Published by The Ecstatic Exchange, 2012)

The Music Space (4/10 – 9/16/2001) (published by The Ecstatic Exchange, 2007)

Where Death Goes (9/20/2001 – 5/1/2002) (published by The Ecstatic Exchange, 2009)

The Flame of Transformation Turns to Light (99 Ghazals Written in English) (5/14 – 8/21/2002) (published by The Ecstatic Exchange, 2007)

Through Rose-Colored Glasses (7/22/2002 – 1/15/2003) (published by The Ecstatic Exchange, 2007)

Psalms for the Broken-Hearted (1/22 – 5/25/2003) (published by The Ecstatic Exchange, 2006)

Hoopoe's Argument (5/27 – 9/18/03)

Love is a Letter Burning in a High Wind (9/21 – 11/6/2003) (published by The Ecstatic Exchange, 2006)

Laughing Buddha/Weeping Sufi (11/7/2003 – 1/10/2004) (published by The Ecstatic Exchange, 2005)

Mars and Beyond (1/20 – 3/29/2004) (published by The Ecstatic Exchange, 2005)

Underwater Galaxies (4/5 – 7/21/2004) (published by The Ecstatic Exchange, 2007)

Cooked Oranges (7/23/2004 – 1/24/2005 (published by The Ecstatic Exchange, 2007)

Holiday from the Perfect Crime (1/25 – 6/11/2005)(published by The Ecstatic Exchange, 2011)

Stories Too Fiery to Sing Too Watery to Whisper (6/13 – 10/24/2005)

Coattails of the Saint (10/26/2005 – 5/10/2006) (published by The Ecstatic Exchange, 2006)

In the Realm of Neither (5/14/2006 – 11/12/06) (published by The Ecstatic Exchange, 2008)

Invention of the Wheel (11/13/06 – 6/10/07)(published by The Ecstatic Exchange, 2010)

The Sound of Geese Over the House (6/15 – 11/4/07)

The Fire Eater's Lunchbreak (11/11/07 – 5/19/2008) (published by The Ecstatic Exchange, 2008)

Sparks Off the Main Strike (5/24/2008 – 1/10/2009)(published by The Ecstatic Exchange, 2010)

Stretched Out on Amethysts (1/13 – 9/17/2009)(published by The Ecstatic Exchange, 2010)

The Throne Perpendicular to All that is Horizontal (9/18/09 – 1/25/10) (published by The Ecstatic Exchange, 2014)

In Constant Incandescence (2/10 – 8/13/10) (published by The Ecstatic Exchange, 2011)

The Caged Bear Spies the Angel (8/30/10 – 3/6/11)(published by The Ecstatic Exchange, 2010)

This Light Slants Upward (3/7 – 10/13/11)

Ramadan is Burnished Sunlight (part of This Light Slants Upward, published separately by The Ecstatic Exchange, 2011)

The Match That Becomes a Conflagration (10/14/11 – 5/9/12)

Down at the Deep End (5/10 – 8/3/12) (published by The Ecstatic Exchange, 2012)

Next Life (8/9/12 – 2/12/13) (published by The Ecstatic Exchange, 2013)

The Soul's Home (2/13 – 10/8/13) (published by The Ecstatic Exchange, 2014)

Eternity Shimmers & Time Holds its Breath (10/10/13 – 1/27/14)

He Comes Running (part of Eternity Shimmers, published as an Ecstatic Exchange Chapbook, 2014)

The Sweet Enigma of it All (1/28/14 –)

www.ingramcontent.com/pod-product-compliance
Lightning Source LLC
Chambersburg PA
CBHW032049150426
43194CB00006B/469